Hard Times

Charles Dickens

Founder Editors: Bill Bowler and Sue Parminter

Text adaptation by Susan Kingsley

Illustrated by Simon Gurr

Charles Dickens (1812–1870) was born in Portsmouth, England, and for most of his life lived in or near London. His family was poor, and he had to go out to work in a factory at the age of twelve. Dickens never forgot this difficult time, and many of his books describe the problems of poor people, especially poor children, and the wide differences between the rich and the poor. When he was older, Dickens started working for a newspaper and then wrote some of the most famous novels in English, including *Hard Times*, *Nicholas Nickleby*, and *A Christmas Carol*, which are also available as Dominoes.

OXFORD
UNIVERSITY PRESS

OXFORD
UNIVERSITY PRESS

Great Clarendon Street, Oxford, OX2 6DP, United Kingdom

Oxford University Press is a department of the University of Oxford.
It furthers the University's objective of excellence in research, scholarship,
and education by publishing worldwide. Oxford is a registered trade
mark of Oxford University Press in the UK and in certain other countries

ISBN: 978 0 19 460821 3   Book
ISBN: 978 0 19 460820 6   Book and Audio Pack

Printed in China

This book is printed on paper from certified and well-managed sources

ACKNOWLEDGEMENTS

Commissioned Illustrations by: Simon Gurr; Ruth Thomlevoid (pp.7, 21, 33, 62, 70)

The publisher would like to thank the following for permission to reproduce photographs:
Alamy Stock Photo pp.6 (Victorian Schoolroom by Charles Keene/Pictorial Press
Ltd), 6 (pupils reciting poetry/North Wind Picture Archives), 63 (Spindrift ship/
World History Archive), 75 (James Fenimore Cooper/Chronicle), 76 (Jane Austen/
Classic Image); Shutterstock pp.74 (Charles Dickens/Everett Historical).

Cover illustration by: Simon Gurr

Contents

BEFORE READING

1 Here are some of the people in the story *Hard Times*. What kind of people are they? Match the sentences with the pictures.

Mr Gradgrind   Tom Gradgrind   Louisa Gradgrind   Mr Harthouse

Mrs Sparsit   Sissy Jupe   Stephen Blackpool   Rachael

a She's serious, clever, and has little love in her life.

b She's nosy, and likes to know everything that's going on.

c She's sweet and very good-hearted.

d She's a poor woman with a hard life.

e He thinks that he's intelligent and interesting.

f He's serious and thinks that time is money.

g He's a hard worker and looks older than he is.

h He likes spending money on clothes, food, and drink.

2 *Hard Times* takes place in a factory town in the north of England in 1870. What kind of problems do the women in the story have, do you think?

Chapter 1
The Gradgrind family

'Now, what I want is facts. Give these boys and girls facts. That's how I teach my own children, and that's how I want you to teach these children here in my school. Facts, Sir, only facts!'

These words were spoken in a large, clean schoolroom with high, white, empty walls. The speaker was Mr Thomas Gradgrind, a **Member of Parliament**, a man of facts, numbers, and information. He had a square body, a square face, and a loud voice. He stood beside the schoolteacher and looked at the children, sitting in rows like empty bottles, all waiting for somebody to fill them up with facts.

'Girl number twenty,' he said, looking at a dark-eyed girl in the front row. 'Who is that girl?'

'Sissy Jupe, Sir,' said girl number twenty, in a shaking voice.

'Sissy is not a name. Call yourself Cecilia.'

'My father calls me Sissy, Sir,' she replied quietly, her face reddening.

'Then tell him that he mustn't. What is your father?'

'He's a **clown** in the **circus**, Sir. The horse-riding circus.'

'We don't want to know about circuses here,' said Gradgrind in a **stern** voice. 'Let me ask you, boys and girls, would you like to have paper on your walls, with pictures of horses on it?'

Half of the children called 'Yes, Sir!' Then the other half, seeing Mr Gradgrind's stony face, shouted 'No, Sir!'

'Of course, no,' said Mr Gradgrind. 'Do you ever, in fact, see real horses walking up and down the sides of rooms? Of course not! And would you like to have a carpet with pictures of flowers on it in your house? Girl number twenty!'

'Yes, Sir,' answered Sissy Jupe, reddening more deeply. 'I like flowers. They're pleasant and pretty. My idea is—'

'Ah! That's the problem!' said Mr Gradgrind. 'Ideas! Never

Member of Parliament a person that the people of a town choose to speak for them in politics

clown a person who wears funny clothes and makes people laugh

circus a travelling show, with clowns, animals, and music

stern very serious

1

have ideas, Cecilia Jupe. Never. Now then, who can tell me what you must have? Bitzer, can you?'

He looked at a boy with very light skin, white hair, and cold, almost colourless eyes.

'Facts, Sir,' replied the boy.

'Very good, Bitzer. You must not have anything which you cannot, in fact, see in the real world – no horses on your walls, no flowers on your floors. Facts, only facts!'

Mr Gradgrind ordered the schoolteacher to begin his lesson, and then left for home.

Stone Lodge, the Gradgrind home, was a mile or two outside Coketown. It was a great square house, with six square windows on each side of the door, and a garden with trees standing in straight, tidy lines. Just like its owner, everything about Stone Lodge was **practical** and sensible.

Mr Gradgrind walked along feeling very pleased with the visit to his school. He wanted it to be a **model** school, and he wanted all the children to be model students, just like his own children. The five little Gradgrinds never filled their heads with the **nonsense** of storybooks, songs, or games. He was, in his own way, a loving father, and had made sure that his children learnt only useful facts from the day that they were born.

As he was walking out of Coketown, Mr Gradgrind suddenly noticed an unpleasant noise. It was music. It was coming from a large, round, wooden building nearby, which had recently appeared on open ground at the edge of the town. From the top flew a brightly coloured flag, on which he read the words *Sleary's Circus*. Notices around the place promised an evening

practical useful and suitable

model a good example for others

nonsense ideas that are not sensible

of fun and excitement with, among others, Mr Jupe and his fantastic dancing dog, Merrylegs.

The very practical Mr Gradgrind continued on his way without taking any notice of this nonsense. But as the road turned, he found himself at the back of the building. There he found a small group of children, all looking through holes in the wooden walls, all trying to catch a **glimpse** of the secrets hidden inside. He put on his glasses, and was **astonished** by what he saw. There, on the dirty grass, was his own model daughter Louisa, and his own model son Tom!

'Louisa! Thomas! What are you doing here?'

Angry and silent, young Tom turned his face away. But Louisa looked her father straight in the eye.

'I was wondering what it was like,' came her short reply.

'Wondering?' he repeated. 'Never wonder, child. Never!'

Louisa was a pretty girl of about fifteen, with the same **sullen** look as her brother. But through her sullenness shone a hungry brightness, like a fire looking for something to burn.

'But why?' asked Mr Gradgrind. 'You and Thomas! With all your facts, all your learning! Why?'

'I was tired, Father. I've been tired for a long time,' she said.

'Tired? Of what?' asked the astonished father.

'I don't know of what – of everything, I think.'

'What will your friends say, Louisa? What will Mr Bounderby say?'

When she heard this name, Louisa stole a look at Mr Gradgrind. It was a look full of meaning and questions, but her father did not see it, and they walked home in silence.

At that same moment, the same Mr Bounderby was standing in front of his friend's fire at Stone Lodge. Bounderby was a big, loud man, a rich banker and factory owner. He was forty-eight, but looked older, and had a great round head like a fat, red ball blown up with air.

'I never had a shoe on my foot or a roof over my head,' he said.

glimpse a quick look

astonished very surprised

sullen silent and angry-looking

dirt something that is not clean

entire whole

ache to hurt

kiss to touch lovingly with your mouth

rub to move your open hand one way and another on something

'I was born in the **dirt** at the side of the road. I was the poorest, sickliest child you have ever seen, Mrs Gradgrind.'

Mrs Gradgrind searched for something to say. She was a thin, pink-eyed little woman, weak in body and in mind. She had no ideas at all, which is why Mr Gradgrind had married her.

'I hope that your mother—' she began.

'My mother? She ran away. Left me alone and hungry,' he said. 'I've never had anyone to help me in my **entire** life.'

Just then, his very practical friend arrived home, with the two sullen-faced young people.

'Oh dear,' said Mrs Gradgrind weakly, when she heard what had happened. 'How could you do this, children? And with my poor head **aching** so badly. Why can't you go and study a bit of ... study some ... why can't you go and study something?'

The children left, and Mr Gradgrind turned to his friend. 'I just can't understand it, Bounderby. How did this nonsense get into their heads? Who gave them these ideas?'

'Wait a moment!' said Mr Bounderby. 'Don't you have one of those circus children in the school?'

'Yes. Cecilia Jupe, by name,' replied Mr Gradgrind.

'Then send her away at once!' shouted Mr Bounderby.

'You are right! Wait while I get her father's address,' answered Mr Gradgrind, going upstairs. While Mr Bounderby was waiting, he opened the door of the children's room.

'It's all right, children,' he said. 'I'll make sure your father won't be angry with you. Well, Louisa, that's worth a **kiss**, isn't it?'

'You can take one, Mr Bounderby,' replied Louisa coldly. Five minutes after Mr Bounderby had gone, she was still **rubbing** her face where he had kissed her.

'What are you doing, Loo?' asked her brother, sullenly. 'You'll rub a hole in your face!'

'You can cut the piece out with a knife, Tom, if you like,' she replied. 'I won't cry!'

READING CHECK

Tick (✔) the boxes to complete the sentences.

a The story begins when ...

1 ☐ Mr Gradgrind is working as a teacher at a model school.

2 ☐ Mr Gradgrind visits his model school and talks to the teachers.

3 ☑ Mr Gradgrind visits his model school and talks to the children.

b Mr Gradgrind thinks that children should ...

1 ☐ dream a little sometimes.

2 ☐ only learn facts.

3 ☐ have their own ideas.

c On his way home, Mr Gradgrind is very surprised ...

1 ☐ to hear music.

2 ☐ to see a wooden circus building at the edge of town.

3 ☐ to see his children looking at the circus.

d Mr Bounderby, the banker, talks to Mrs Gradgrind ...

1 ☐ about the happy times he had when he was a child.

2 ☐ about the hard times he is living through at the moment.

3 ☐ about the hard times he had when he was younger.

e Mr Bounderby thinks that Sissy Jupe ...

1 ☐ puts bad ideas in the heads of the school children.

2 ☐ should study more.

3 ☐ should go to live with Mr Gradgrind's family.

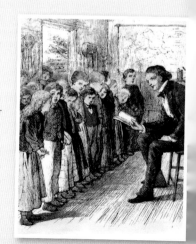

f When Mr Bounderby wants to kiss her, Louisa ...

1 ☐ lets him do it, but hates it.

2 ☐ doesn't let him do it.

3 ☐ lets him do it because she likes him.

WORD WORK

Use the words in the horses to complete the sentences.

clown/ circus

kissed/ rubs

entire/ dirt

nonsense/ stern

model/ practical

parliament/ member

astonished/ glimpse

sullenly/ aching

a Thomas Gradgrind is a _Member_ of _Parliament_.

b Sissy Jupe's father is a .... in Mr Sleary's ....

c Mr Gradgrind is a .... unsmiling man who doesn't like ....

d Mr Gradgrind has a .... school where students learn .... things.

e When Mr Gradgrind catches a .... of Tom and Louisa looking at the circus, he is ....

f Mr Bounderby says that he was born in the .... by the road and never had any help in his .... life.

g Mrs Gradgrind's head is .... and Tom and Louisa go off .... to study.

h With her hand Louisa .... the place where Mr Bounderby .... her.

GUESS WHAT

What happens in the next chapter? Tick (✔) two boxes.

a ☐ Sissy Jupe's father dies.

b ☐ Sissy Jupe's father runs away from the circus.

c ☐ Tom runs away to be in the circus.

d ☐ Louisa and Tom go to live with Mr Bounderby.

e ☐ Mr Gradgrind asks Sissy to come and live at his house.

Coketown was a town built on Fact. It was a town of machines and tall chimneys, and of red **brick**, blackened by years of endless smoke and dirt. The streets were all like each other, and people, all the same, went in and out at the same time every day. High buildings, full of windows, shook all day long with the noise of their great machines, and every week, every year, was just the same as the one before.

Mr Gradgrind and Mr Bounderby were walking through these streets, when a young girl suddenly ran past them, carrying a large bottle.

'Stop there, girl number twenty!' called Mr Gradgrind. 'Where are you going in that great hurry?'

'I'm taking this to father, Sir,' replied the girl.

'Drink!' said Mr Bounderby, looking at the bottle in her hand.

'Oh, no, Sir!' answered the girl. 'It's Nine **Oils**. To rub father with. Our people always use it when they get hurt in the **ring**.'

'Lazy, useless people,' said Mr Bounderby.

She looked up at him, astonished and fearful. Then Mr Gradgrind spoke to her more kindly.

'We're going to your father's house. Can you take us there?'

Sissy took them to a blackened building, through a small, **shabby** bar, and up some dark, narrow stairs.

'It's up here, Sir,' she said. 'If you hear a dog, it's only Merrylegs.'

They found themselves in a shabby little room.

'Father isn't here, Sir,' said Sissy, with great surprise. She offered her visitors two chairs to sit on, and hurriedly left the room. From the floors above, they could hear doors opening and closing, and sounds of surprised voices. Then she ran back into the room, and threw open a large, old suitcase. It was empty.

'He's gone to the ring,' she cried, her eyes full of fear. 'He must be there. I'll get him at once!' She then disappeared down the

brick square stones for building walls and houses

oil a thick liquid that is sometimes used in medicines or to help machines to work

ring the circle where circus people dance, sing, and ride

shabby old and poor-looking

stairs, her long hair flying behind her.

As the news passed through the building, people from Sleary's company came to join the two men in the room. There were men, women, and children; kind, gentle people, caring for each other like one large family. Last came Sleary himself, a short, fat man, with one glass eye, and a voice that was **worn out** from a lifetime of shouting in the ring.

'Jupe can't do it any more,' said one voice. 'He's getting too old.'

'He's left her, but she won't believe it. They were like one person, that father and daughter, always together.'

'He always wanted the best **education** for the girl – he was so happy when she got into the school.'

Suddenly Sissy ran back into the room. She saw the faces of the people there, gave a heart-breaking cry, and fell into the arms of the woman nearest to her. The woman held her, cried with her, and **comforted** her.

'Look here, girl, what's your name?' said Mr Bounderby, in a loud, stern voice. 'Can't you see? Your father's left you. You're not going to see him again, and that's that.'

The circus people looked at Bounderby, and words passed between them. Then Mr Gradgrind stood up and spoke to Sissy.

'I have a **proposal**, Jupe. I will give you an education and take care of you. But you must decide at once if you want to come or not.

worn out very tired from being used a lot

education teaching

comfort to make somebody feel happier

proposal a plan or an idea about how to do something

Also, if you come with me, you must never speak to any of the people in this room again. It is you who must choose, but remember: a good practical education is a very important thing in life. I understand that even your father felt this.'

At these last words, Sissy stopped crying, and turned her face to Mr Gradgrind.

'But when Father comes back – how will he find me?'

'Do not worry, Jupe,' replied Mr Gradgrind calmly. 'He will come to Mr Sleary here, who will write to me.'

The circus women then packed Sissy's few clothes for her, and one by one her friends came to kiss her goodbye.

'Leave the bottle, my dear,' said Mr Sleary, seeing that the Nine Oils was still held tightly to her chest.

'No, no!' she cried. 'It's for Father when he comes back!'

'Very well, then. Goodbye, my dear. Be good, and don't forget us,' he said, and turning to Mr Gradgrind he added: 'And you too, Sir, think the best of us, not the worst. People can't work all the time, they need to be amused, too. Think the best of us, not the worst.'

———

And so began Sissy Jupe's new life. But it was not an easy one for her. At school, facts rained down hard on her all day long. Mr Gradgrind, **disappointed** that she was so slow to learn, turned the wheel of the learning machine faster. This made Sissy quieter and unhappier, but not any cleverer.

At Stone Lodge, Sissy took care of weak Mrs Gradgrind. Here too, her daily life went round like an endless machine, with little place for friendliness or conversation. Then, one evening Sissy turned to Louisa and said: 'Oh, Miss Louisa, I am so stupid. I try to get the answers right at school, but I always seem to say the wrong things.'

'Did your father know many things?' asked Louisa.

Mr Gradgrind had told Sissy never to speak of her earlier life, and she was almost afraid to answer. But Louisa began to ask

disappointed
unhappy because you don't get what you want

more and more questions, with a wild and hungry interest. So Sissy told her about her loving father, their life in the travelling circus, and about the wonderful storybooks she used to read with him. And Louisa, against all her parents' wishes, began to wonder.

After that, every time that Sissy asked Mr Gradgrind, 'Please, Sir – have you had a letter for me yet?' Louisa was as **anxious** as Sissy was to hear his answer. And when, as always, the answer was 'No' Louisa felt almost as sad and disappointed as Sissy did. And Louisa began to think that perhaps Hope really could be as strong as Fact.

anxious worried and excited

READING CHECK

Are these sentences true or false? Tick (✔) the boxes.

		True	False
a	Mr Gradgrind and Mr Bounderby are looking for Sissy when they see her in the street.	☐	☑
b	Sissy has bought her father a bottle of medicine because he is hurt.	☐	☐
c	When they arrive in Sissy's room, Sissy runs off to look for Merrylegs.	☐	☐
d	Sissy's father has left because he's too old to work in the circus any longer.	☐	☐
e	Mr Gradgrind asks Sissy to go and live with his family.	☐	☐
f	Sissy finds her new life with the Gradgrinds easy.	☐	☐
g	Louisa Gradgrind becomes interested in Sissy's stories of her past life.	☐	☐

WORD WORK

1 Find words from Chapter 2 in the smoke.

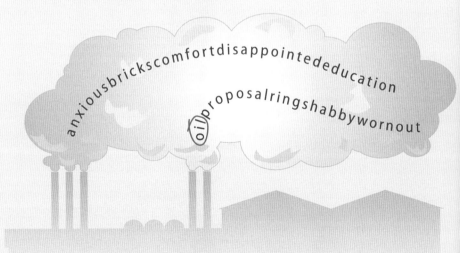

anxiousbrickscomfortdisappointededucation(oi)proposalringshabbywornout

2 Complete these sentences with words from Activity 1.

a Sissy is taking a bottle of o i l to her father to rub him with.

b Most of the houses in Coketown are made of red _ _ _ _ _ _.

c Sissy and her father live in an old and _ _ _ _ _ _ house.

d Circus people use Nine Oils when they hurt themselves in the _ _ _ _.

e Mr Jupe is _ _ _ _ _ _ _ and can't work any more.

f Mr Jupe was happy that Sissy was getting a good _ _ _ _ _ _ _ _ _ _ at Mr Gradgrind's school.

g When Sissy cries, the circus people _ _ _ _ _ _ _ _ her.

h Mr Gradgrind has an interesting _ _ _ _ _ _ _ _ _ for Sissy.

i Later he feels _ _ _ _ _ _ _ _ _ _ _ _ when he discovers that Sissy is a slow learner.

j For weeks Sissy is very _ _ _ _ _ _ _ for news of her father.

GUESS WHAT

| Stephen Blackpool | Mr Bounderby | Rachael | Mrs Sparsit |

What happens in the next chapter? Match the people with the sentences.

a .... and .... work at one of the factories in Coketown.

b .... owns factories in Coketown.

c .... has been unhappily married for many years.

d .... looks after Mr Bounderby's house.

e .... and .... have been close friends for a long time.

f .... doesn't want to help a poor worker.

g .... was once richer than she is now.

Chapter 3
Stephen Blackpool

In the smoky heart of Coketown, with its thick, unhealthy air, and its narrow, blackened streets, there lived a man called Stephen Blackpool. He had had a hard life, and with his worried face and thin grey hair, he looked older than his forty years. Stephen was a cotton **weaver**, one of many thousands of workers, or 'Hands', who turned the great machines of Coketown. He was a good weaver, and a **simple**, honest man.

It was a cold, wet night. There were no more lights. The great factory fell dark, and the bell had rung to say that the Hands' working day was over. Stephen stood in the street and watched the groups of young woman as they passed on their way home from work. At last they were all gone.

'I've missed Rachael,' he said to himself and, disappointed, turned to go home. But then he recognized the shape of a woman, walking alone along the rainy street. Stephen walked faster to catch up with her, and called: 'Rachael!'

Rachael turned, showing a quiet, gentle face. She was a woman of thirty-five, with very gentle, dark eyes, and shining hair.

'Ah, it's you, Stephen,' she said, smiling at him. They walked along together for a while.

'It's better if we don't walk too much together,' she said.

'It's hard,' said Stephen. 'But you're right. People might talk. You've been a true friend, Rachael, over so many years. For me your word is **law**. A good law. Better than some real ones.'

'Try not to think about it, Stephen,' she said, softly.

When they came close to Rachael's home, she touched his hand gently and wished him good night. He watched her disappear down the narrow street, and then he went on his way. The clouds had gone now, the moon shone, and it seemed that the man, like the night, had brightened.

weaver a person who makes cotton into cloth

simple natural and not wanting many things

law something that tells you what you must or must not do

Stephen's own home was a room over a little shop. It was small, with simple furniture, but tidy and clean. As he entered the darkened room he suddenly fell against something on the floor. It was a woman – but what an awful woman! She was unwashed, **drunk** and helpless, with **stained** clothes, and long dirty hair falling over her dirty face.

'You're back again, woman,' cried Stephen.

'Yes, back again and again! And why not?' screamed the woman. 'Come away from the bed, it's mine!'

She threw herself heavily on the bed, and was soon asleep. Stephen hid her body and face with a blanket, then sat down in a chair and slept.

At lunchtime the next day, when the bell rang and the great machines fell silent, Stephen stepped out of the hot factory and into a cold, rainy wind. He looked worn out, with deep lines on his tired face. Taking only a little bread, he turned away from the

drunk when someone has had too much beer or other strong drink

stained with dirt on it

narrow dirty streets of the workers' side of town, and walked up the hill to the house of the factory-owner. Stephen went up the two white steps to the door of the red brick house and read the name on the square metal plate there. BOUNDERBY, it said in large metal letters, very like the man himself. He rang the bell.

Mr Bounderby was sitting at his lunch table drinking sweet **wine**. 'What's the matter with you?' he asked when Stephen was brought into the room. Stephen looked for a moment at Mr Bounderby's **housekeeper**, Mrs Sparsit.

'I can go, Mr Bounderby, if you wish,' said Mrs Sparsit.

With his mouth still full of meat, Mr Bounderby held up a hand to tell Mrs Sparsit to stay. He ate the mouthful, and then turned to Stephen.

'Now you know, this good lady is a grand lady, a high lady from a fine family. Sadly, she has fallen on hard times and now keeps house for me, but she was, in her early days, at the very top of the tree. So, if what you have to say is suitable for the ears of a true lady, then this lady will stay where she is.'

'I hope I've never said anything in my life which isn't suitable for a true lady to hear, Sir,' answered Stephen.

'Well, go on then,' said Bounderby.

'Sir, I've come to ask for your help,' began Stephen. 'I've been married for nineteen years, nineteen long, hard years. When I married, my wife was young, pretty enough, and not a bad girl. But she went bad – soon.'

'I've heard all this before,' said Bounderby. 'She began to drink, stopped working, and sold all the furniture.'

'I wasn't an unkind husband, Sir, I tried to help her, I tried everything. But she came back, again and again, drunk and angry, and things went from bad to worse.'

'Well, then? What have you come to say?' asked Bounderby, bringing another large forkful of meat to his lips.

'I can't live like this any more, Sir. I wanted to ask you how I can be free of her.'

'What are you talking about?' replied Mr Bounderby.

'I have read, Sir, that some grand people can end their **marriages**, if they wish to. Isn't there a law that can help me?'

'There is a law, but it isn't for people like you. It costs money. A lot of money. Two or three thousand pounds, maybe.'

'So what can I do?'

'Nothing!' shouted Bounderby, standing up in front of a large **painting** of his own fat, red face on the wall. 'You took that woman to be your wife and, good or bad, you have to stay with her. You Hands are all the same. If you're given a chance you'll ask for fine horses and gold spoons, too. Gold spoons, I say!'

'Thank you, Sir. I wish you good day,' said Stephen, shaking his head sadly, and leaving the house.

As Stephen was crossing the street, he felt somebody touch him on the arm. It was an old woman, cleanly and simply dressed, but with the dirt of the country on her shoes.

'Excuse me, Sir,' began the woman. 'Didn't I see you just now, coming out of that **gentleman's** house?'

marriage when two people are married

painting a picture, done with different colours and brushes

gentleman a man from a good family, usually rich

'Yes, Madam, that was me,' replied Stephen.

'How did he look? Was he well? Was he strong and healthy?'

Stephen answered 'Yes' to these questions, and the woman thanked him, her face shining with happiness.

'I see you're from the country,' said Stephen.

'I am. I walked nine miles to the station this morning, then came forty miles by train, and I'll go back the same way this afternoon. I save my money and come once a year. I walk in the streets and try to catch a glimpse of that gentleman,' said the woman, pointing towards Mr Bounderby's house.

She walked with Stephen as far as the factory. They arrived just as the bell rang for the start of the afternoon's work.

'What a beautiful bell! What a fine factory! You must be so happy to work here, Sir!' cried the woman, kissing his hand.

Stephen returned to his work, to the heat, the noise and the smoke of the factory. When at last night fell, the bell rang again, the machines stopped, and Stephen went out into the dark, wet streets. He waited again for Rachael, but she did not come. How he missed her kind face and soft voice! Hers was the only face which could brighten his darkness, hers was the only voice which could comfort him in his troubles.

No word of a new marriage had ever passed between them, but he knew that if he was free to ask her, she'd like to marry him. As he walked home, he thought of all the lost years, the best years of his life, which he had spent tied to that terrible woman. And he thought of Rachael, who had been so young when they first met, and who was now growing old. He thought of all the girls she had seen marry and have children, while she lived her quiet, lonely life – for him. Sometimes he had seen a sadness in her gentle face, and it filled him with pain.

When he entered his room he found peace and quiet there. His wife lay unmoving in bed, while Rachael sat on a chair next to her. Rachael turned her head, and the light of her face shone into the midnight of his mind.

'She's hurt, Stephen. She needed help.'

Rachael put a few drops from a bottle on a piece of cotton, and **wiped** it gently over the cuts on the woman's face and neck. He followed Rachael's hands with his eyes, and read what was written on the bottle. A drink from that bottle meant immediate death.

'I'll stay another few hours,' said Rachael softly. 'Now you sit down and try to sleep. You look so white and tired.'

To please her, Stephen did as Rachael said, and slowly his eyes closed and he began to dream. After a while he could hear the wind blowing and the rain beating on the window. The room looked the same. The fire had gone out, and Rachael seemed to be sleeping. Then the body on the bed moved, and the woman looked around, with wild, crazy eyes. She reached out a hand, took the bottle, and pulled the **stopper** out with her teeth.

Stephen watched, but could not move or speak, not knowing if he was awake or dreaming. The woman took the stopper from her mouth and held the bottle up to her lips – ready to drink from it. But at that moment Rachael woke, and pulled the bottle from her.

'Rachael, am I waking or dreaming this awful night?' he cried.

'It's all right, Stephen,' she replied, emptying the bottle into the fireplace. 'She's quiet now. She'll be better in the morning.'

With a broken voice, she wished Stephen goodnight, and disappeared into a night which was now still, and bright with stars.

wipe to make something clean with a cloth

stopper something that you put into the top of a bottle to close it

ACTIVITIES

READING CHECK

Correct nine more mistakes in the chapter summary.

Stephen Blackpool works in one of the Coketown factories as a ~~cleaner~~ *weaver*. He is an

honest man and has had a happy life. One evening, on his way to work, he meets his

friend Rachael and walks with her. When he gets home he finds his sister in his

room. She is drunk and she screams at him and then goes to work. At lunchtime the

next day Stephen visits Mr Bounderby at work to ask for his help. He asks how he

can end his marriage. Mr Bounderby wants to help. As Stephen leaves, an old

woman stops him. She is from the country and has come to Coketown for the day.

She is interested in Mr Gradgrind's life. On his way home after work Stephen thinks

about Louisa. When he gets to Rachael's house, she is there with his wife, who is

asleep. Stephen goes to sleep and wakes up to see that his wife is going to drink

something dangerous from a bottle. He takes the bottle from her and leaves.

WORD WORK

1 Correct the words in these sentences. They all come from Chapter 3.
a Stephen is a very dimple man. *simple*
b He never does anything that is against the paw . ...
c His wife comes home trunk one day. ....
d Mr Bounderby says that a carriage is for life. ....
e Rachael wires Mrs Blackpool's face with some cotton. ....

2 These words don't match the pictures. Correct them.

a ~~gentleman~~

...painting...

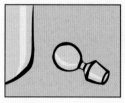

b stained

....

c housekeeper

....

d painting

....

e weaver

....

f stopper

....

GUESS WHAT

What happens in the next chapter? Tick (✔) the boxes.

a ☐ Tom
☐ Mr Gradgrind   ... works for Mr Bounderby.
☐ Sissy

b ☐ Mrs Sparsit
☐ Sissy   ... agrees to get married to Mr Bounderby.
☐ Louisa

c Mr Gradgrind is pleased with ...   ☐ Louisa.
☐ Tom.
☐ Sissy.

spark a very
small piece of fire

selfish thinking
only about yourself

Time went on in Coketown like the turning of its machines. The years passed, and Thomas Gradgrind saw that his daughter Louisa was now a young woman.

'My dear Louisa, I must speak to you alone and seriously,' he said to her one evening. 'Come to my room after breakfast tomorrow, will you?'

'Yes, Father,' she replied.

Mr Gradgrind kissed his daughter, and went out for the evening. Louisa returned to her room, where she sat, looking quietly at the **sparks** of the dying fire.

'Are you there, Loo?' called her brother, looking round the door. Tom was now a tall young man, working at Bounderby's Bank, and living at Bounderby's house. Free of his parents at last, he now enjoyed all the pleasures which the town could offer a young gentleman. As sullen and **selfish** as he had always been, Tom continued to look after his only true interest – himself.

'Dear Tom,' she answered, standing up and kissing him. 'How long is it since you've been to see me?'

'Well, old Bounderby keeps me quite busy. But if he tries to push me too hard, I say "My sister Loo will be disappointed and hurt, Mr Bounderby. She always used to tell me you would be easier with me than this." That one always works well with him!'

Tom waited for a reply, but none came.

'I say, Loo! Has Father said anything special to you today?'

'No, but he told me he wished to talk to me in the morning.'

'Ah, that's what I mean,' said Tom. 'Do you know where Father is tonight? Well, I'll tell you – he's with old Bounderby at the Bank, having a good talk, far away from his housekeeper Mrs Sparsit's ears.'

Tom suddenly put his arm round his sister's **waist**.

'You do care about me, don't you, Loo?' he asked.

'I do, Tom, although you don't come to see me often enough.'

'Well, my dear sister, being together with you is so **jolly**, I'd like it if we could be together more, wouldn't you? If you decided to say yes to something, I know, Loo, it could happen!'

Louisa continued to look silently into the fire.

'Well, I wanted to come and let you know what's happening. You won't forget how much you care about me, will you, Loo?'

'No, dear Tom, I won't forget.'

'That's **splendid**. Goodbye, then.'

Louisa went with him to the door, from where she could see the fires of Coketown. She stood there for a long time, looking into a night sky burning with fiery red sparks, and wondered what the future held for her.

———

The next morning Louisa appeared in her father's room. Its walls were filled with books, whose pages contained enough facts and numbers to answer all the world's problems. It was a hard, serious room, with a large clock whose deadly 'tick, tock' counted the seconds from life to death.

waist the narrow part in the middle of your body

jolly happy and fun

splendid very good

'My dear Louisa,' said Mr Gradgrind. 'You have received a proposal of marriage.'

Louisa said nothing. Her father repeated his words, to which she replied, in a voice without any **emotion**: 'I am listening, Father. Please go on.'

'My child, I must tell you that Mr Bounderby has, for many years, been looking forward to the day when he could offer you his hand in marriage. And now this day has come.'

There was silence between them. The hands of the clock moved heavily, and Mr Gradgrind began to feel uncomfortable.

'Father,' she said at last. 'Do you think I love Mr Bounderby?'

'My dear, I really cannot say.'

'Father,' continued Louisa in the same emotionless voice. 'Does Mr Bounderby ask me to love him?'

'Well, my child, that is a difficult question. Perhaps because the word which you use is not a suitable one.'

'Which word should I use, then?'

'Louisa, my dear, you are not one of these girls who fill their heads with stories and nonsense. You are a sensible, practical person. You should think about this question in the same way as any other question – by simply looking at the Facts.'

Louisa's eyes turned towards the window.

'Are you asking the chimneys of Coketown to decide for you?' asked Mr Gradgrind.

'It looks like there is only slow, **monotonous** smoke,' she replied, turning quickly. 'But at night, fiery sparks shoot out, Father!'

'I know that, Louisa. I do not see what it has to do with the question,' said her father, who really did not understand at all.

'Father, I have often thought that life is short. And while I live, I wish to do what I can, although it is not much. So, as Mr Bounderby asks me to marry him in this way, I accept his proposal. What does it matter?'

'Louisa, perhaps I ought to ask you something. Have you, in

emotion strong feeling

monotonous never changing and boring

secret, received any other proposal?'

'How could I, Father?' she answered. 'Who have I seen? Where have I been? What do I know of tastes, ideas, emotions?'

'Very true, very true,' agreed the very practical parent.

'You taught me so well, Father, that I've never had a child's heart, never felt a child's fear, or dreamed a child's dream.'

What a model daughter! And so grateful for the success of her education! The **proud** father kissed his **eldest** child, and took her to tell his wife the happy news.

Mrs Gradgrind kissed her daughter weakly, and wished her a marriage with better health than her own. Sissy, working at Mrs Gradgrind's side, looked wordlessly at Louisa. It was a look of many emotions – surprise, sadness, **pity**. Louisa's face was **impassive**. She did not turn her eyes to Sissy, but she knew that the look was there.

Eight weeks later, Mr Bounderby and Miss Gradgrind were married. On the day of her practical, well-arranged wedding, just as Louisa was leaving Stone Lodge to begin her new life, she met her brother at the bottom of the stairs. His face was red, either with emotion or with wine from the wedding dinner.

'You're a fine girl, Loo,' whispered Tom. 'And a splendid sister! Won't life be jolly now!'

proud happy about something that you have done

eldest oldest of three or more children

pity the feeling of being sorry for someone because they have problems

impassive not moving

READING CHECK

1 Put these sentences in the correct order. Number them 1–10.

a ☐ Louisa and Mr Bounderby get married.

b ☐ Sissy is surprised by the news of the marriage.

c ☐ Mr Gradgrind goes out for the evening.

d ☐ Tom tells Louisa that it could be jolly if they are together more.

e ☐ Tom visits Louisa.

f ☐ Louisa agrees to marry Mr Bounderby although she doesn't love him.

g ☐ Mr Gradgrind tells Louisa that he wants to talk to her.

h 1 Mr Gradgrind tells Louisa that Mr Bounderby has proposed to her.

i ☐ Mr Gradgrind feels proud of his practical daughter.

j ☐ Louisa goes to her father's room.

2 Are these sentences true or false? Tick (✔) the boxes.

	True	False
a Tom only comes to see Louisa when he wants something from her.	✔	☐
b Tom talks to Mr Bounderby about Louisa in order to make Mr Bounderby nicer to him.	☐	☐
c Tom tells Louisa that Mr Bounderby wants to marry her.	☐	☐
d Tom wants Louisa to marry Mr Bounderby because he hopes that – as the wife of his employer – she can help him.	☐	☐
e Mr Gradgrind thinks that love is very important in a marriage.	☐	☐
f Louisa thinks of herself like factory smoke, by day boring and grey, but at night full of emotional fire.	☐	☐
g Mrs Gradgrind hopes that Louisa's life will be like her own.	☐	☐
h Sissy is happy that Louisa is going to marry Mr Bounderby.	☐	☐

ACTIVITIES

WORD WORK

Find the words to complete the sentences.

a Louisa spends long hours looking at the _sparks_ in the fire. krasps

b Tom is only interested in himself and is _ _ _ _ _ _ _. lesshif

c Tom thinks that living with Louisa will be _ _ _ _ _. yojll

d Louisa shows no feelings about her marriage to Mr Bounderby – she is _ _ _ _ _ _ _ _ _. vispimase

e Louisa is Mr Gradgrind's _ _ _ _ _ _ child. steeld

f Louisa's life in Coketown isn't interesting; it's _ _ _ _ _ _ _ _ _ _ _. moonoutson

g Mr Gradgrind is _ _ _ _ _ because Louisa is a model child. dropu

h Sissy feels _ _ _ _ for Louisa because she is marrying someone that she doesn't love. ityp

i Louisa speaks to her father in a voice with no _ _ _ _ _ _ _. inotome

j Tom is very pleased with his sister and thinks she is _ _ _ _ _ _ _ _. dipslend

k When Tom is friendly with Louisa, he puts his arm round her _ _ _ _ _. stwai

GUESS WHAT

What happens in the next chapter? Tick (✔) three boxes.

a ☐ A new and interesting man arrives in Coketown.

b ☐ Sissy falls in love with the new man.

c ☐ Mrs Sparsit has moved out of Mr Bounderby's house now that he is married.

d ☐ Bitzer, an old student from Gradgrind's school, now works at Bounderby's Bank.

e ☐ Tom loses his job at Bounderby's Bank.

f ☐ Louisa's feelings for her brother change.

Chapter 5
A visitor to Coketown

It was a hot summer afternoon. A hard, bright sun shone through the dark smoke of Coketown, and the smell of hot oil filled its thick, dirty air.

On the cooler side of a quiet street walked a **handsome** man of about thirty-five, tall and expensively dressed, clearly a stranger to Coketown. As he passed Bounderby's Bank, a large red brick building like so many others, he was noticed by a pair of eyes at the window. The little black eyes, and long pointed nose between them, belonged to Mrs Sparsit. The grand lady had lived there for a year now, since the marriage of Mr Bounderby, when she had politely accepted her employer's offer of rooms at the Bank. She had spent the year looking down her long nose at the banker himself with the greatest pity.

The handsome stranger went on his way, and Mrs Sparsit turned to her tea and cakes. These were brought to her by Bitzer, who now worked for Mr Bounderby, and also lived at the Bank. He was a cold young man, with very white skin and colourless eyes. Indeed, Bitzer had changed very little since his days as Mr Gradgrind's model student, when he had helped to explain to girl number twenty about 'Facts, only Facts.'

'Thank you, Bitzer,' said Mrs Sparsit, taking her cup of tea in her hand. 'And how was the day? Has everyone been working well?'

'Yes, Madam,' replied Bitzer. 'All except for young Mr Tom Gradgrind, Madam. I don't like his ways at all.'

Bitzer was also the office spy, and received some money each Christmas for doing this extra job.

'Bitzer,' said the lady. 'What did I say about using names?'

'I'm sorry, Madam. All except for – one **individual**.'

'Ah,' she said over her teacup, now agreeing to listen.

'This one individual. He hasn't done an honest day's work since he came here. He's lazy and **extravagant**, and only keeps his job

handsome
good-looking

individual
person

extravagant
spending too
much money

28

because he has a friend in a high place. And she gives him money, and he spends it in extravagant ways and **gambles** with it.'

'Ah,' said Mrs Sparsit, shaking her head sadly, and turning her eyes back to the now empty street.

———————

Later that afternoon, the well-dressed visitor arrived at Mr Bounderby's house, carrying a letter with these words on it:

To Mr Josiah Bounderby of Coketown, specially to introduce Mr James Harthouse.

Thomas Gradgrind

'So you're not from these parts, Sir,' said Mr Bounderby to Mr Harthouse. 'Well, let me tell you about the place. First of all – our smoke. It is the best thing in the world, our smoke – excellent for the health. And then there are our factories. Working in our factories is the lightest and easiest work there is, and the best paid. But those Hands, they're all trying to get fine meat and gold spoons, every one of them! But I tell you, they're not going to get it from me! None of them!'

'Quite right, Mr Bounderby,' agreed Mr Harthouse.

'I see you're a gentleman, a man of good family,' went on Bounderby. 'Well, I'm Josiah Bounderby of Coketown, and I don't care about fine families. I'm a simple man. I was born with nothing, the poorest of the poor. My own mother **abandoned** me. Everything I have today I got through my own hard work, and I'm proud of it. So I'll shake hands with you, man to man. How are you?'

'Very well, Sir, thanks to the healthy air of Coketown,' replied the gentleman, in his easy, careless way.

Mr Bounderby invited his visitor to meet his wife, and took him into their **drawing room**. Mr Harthouse had never seen

gamble to play games for money

abandon to leave someone; to stop visiting or using a place

drawing room a living room in a large house

a girl like Louisa Bounderby before. She appeared so cold and proud, but was clearly ashamed of her husband's **boastful** ways. Her face was handsome, but showed no emotion. All her feelings seemed to be locked up inside her. She did not seem happy, but there was a calmness about her. Her body was with them, but her mind was far away. James Harthouse then turned to look at the room itself. It was a rich room, but hard and comfortless. He saw nothing soft or pretty about the place, nothing touched by womanly gentleness.

'I understand that you wish to become a Member of Parliament like my father,' said Mrs Bounderby. 'And that you hope to help the country out of its problems.'

'Oh no,' laughed Harthouse. 'I won't pretend to do that! One man's ideas or another man's ideas – it's all the same to me.'

'Have you no ideas of your own?' she asked.

'Not any more,' he replied, in his careless way. 'I've seen a lot of the world, and I'm bored with it all. Life's monotonous. Nothing's worth anything. So what does it matter?'

At six-thirty Mr Harthouse sat down to dinner with Mr and Mrs Bounderby, at a table with a fourth empty place. As he made polite replies to Mr Bounderby's endless talk, he looked from time to time at Louisa.

'Is there nothing,' he wondered, 'that will move that face?'

boastful talking importantly about yourself

Yes! There was something, and here it was. Tom appeared. As the door opened, Louisa's face changed, and she turned to give her brother a most beautiful smile.

treat to speak and act towards

plentiful a lot of

'Ah, so this sullen young thing is all she cares for,' thought James Harthouse. 'What loneliness must be in her heart.'

During the dinner he watched the ungrateful and uncaring way Tom **treated** his sister. But Harthouse was open and friendly towards Tom, and when he said that he was unsure of his way back to his hotel, young Gradgrind immediately offered to go with him.

Arriving at the hotel, Mr Harthouse invited Tom up to his room, where the armchairs were soft, the wine was good and **plentiful**, and the conversation was easy. Tom soon felt very lazy and comfortable indeed, smoked and drank happily, and talked freely to Mr Harthouse. He told the gentleman about his sister Loo, who had accepted her first and only marriage proposal, not because she had any love for 'old Bounderby', but because she wanted to help her brother. Mr Harthouse listened with great interest, and Tom stayed late into the night. When he finally went on his sleepy way home, Tom felt sure that he had just made an excellent new friend.

READING CHECK

Match the sentences with the people in the pictures.

1 Mr Harthouse

2 Mrs Sparsit

3 Tom

4 Bitzer

5 Louisa

6 Mr Bounderby

a `2` ... sees Mr Harthouse walking past the bank.

b ☐ ... tells Mrs Sparsit the office secrets.

c ☐ ... gives money to Tom to help him.

d ☐ ... has a letter that introduces him to Mr Bounderby.

e ☐ ... tells Mr Harthouse about good Coketown factories and bad Coketown workers.

f ☐ ... finds Louisa very interesting.

g ☐ ... talks to Mr Harthouse about being a Member of Parliament.

h ☐ ... is the only person who can make Louisa smile.

i ☐ ... invites Tom to his room to talk about his sister.

WORD WORK

Use the words from the cakes on page 33 to complete the sentences.

a Mr Harthouse is a _handsome_ man.

b Tom loses lots of money when he .... on horses or at cards.

c Mr Bounderby is a .... man. He's always talking importantly about the things that he does.

d Louisa .... Tom very nicely, but he isn't very nice to her.

e Mr Bounderby says that his mother .... him when he was a baby.

f The drinks and cigarettes in Mr Harthouse's room are ....

g Tom isn't a very hard-working ....

h Tom is very .... – always spending his money in different ways.

i Mr Harthouse first meets Louisa in the .... room at Mr Bounderby's house.

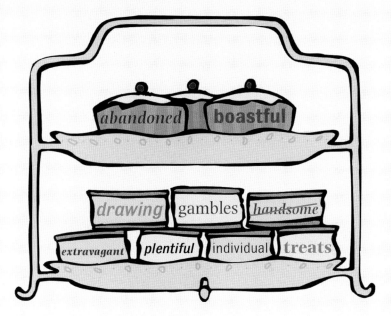

abandoned boastful drawing gambles handsome extravagant plentiful individual treats

GUESS WHAT

What happens in the next chapter? Match the first and second parts of these sentences.

a Stephen Blackpool ...

b Bitzer asks Stephen ...

c Bounderby decides that he should ...

d The old lady from the country asks Stephen ...

e Louisa and Tom ...

f Tom tells Stephen ...

1 to go to Mr Bounderby's house.

2 about Mrs Bounderby.

3 that he wants to help him.

4 tell Stephen to leave his job at the factory.

5 has problems at work.

6 come to visit Stephen at home.

Old and grey at forty, Stephen Blackpool had troubles not only at home, but at work, too.

There had come to Coketown a man by the name of Slackbridge, a man with a fiery face and a loud, **hoarse** voice. This Slackbridge had brought the Coketown workers together, and he shouted strong and angry words at them. He called them 'my friends and brothers', and shouted, his **fist** held high, that it was time to join the **Union**. 'Yes!' shouted the Coketown Hands, all except for one. For Stephen could see that, among all the hundreds of men in the room, Slackbridge was the least honest and the least manly. He refused to follow him. He stood up in front of the other workers, spoke simply and honestly to them of how he felt, and then walked out of the room.

The next days were the loneliest of Stephen's life. He went to and from his work as usual, but not a single person spoke to him. When he went into the street, the other workers crossed the road to walk on the other side.

One evening, as Stephen was leaving the factory, he was stopped by a young man with very light skin, hair, and eyes.

'You're Blackpool, aren't you?' said the young man.

'Yes,' replied Stephen, **blushing** to hear another person's voice.

'Mr Bounderby wants to speak to you,' said Bitzer. 'You can find the house yourself, can't you? It'll save me the walk.'

Stephen said that he could, and turned his steps towards the large red brick house on the hill. He knocked on the big black door, and was taken into the drawing room. Around the tea-table sat Mr Bounderby, his young wife, her brother, and a grand gentleman from London. Stephen stood by the door, his hat in his hand.

'Well,' said Mr Bounderby, his voice like a loud wind. 'Tell us about yourself and this Union.'

'I'm sorry, Sir, but I have nothing to say about it.'

hoarse sounding hard from too much shouting

fist a hand with the fingers closed

union a group of workers who join together to try to make the workplace better

blush to become red in the face because you are shy or embarrassed

'You see, Harthouse,' said Mr Bounderby, speaking to the gentleman at his side. 'The man's afraid to open his lips about them. They're a lot of criminals, every one of them.'

Stephen, seeing Louisa's friendly face watching him closely, turned and spoke his next words to her instead of Mr Bounderby. 'Madam, I've lived and worked beside these men all my life, and I tell you, they are not criminals.'

'So, Blackpool, you have nothing to say about the Union men,' continued Mr Bounderby, his wind blowing stronger. 'Then tell us, what are you people **complaining** about?'

Stephen looked unsure for a moment, then spoke.

'Look around this town, Sir, this great rich town. See the numbers of people here, working all their lives, all in the same way, from when they are born until they die. Look at how many we are, and how we live. The factories go on day after day, we work day after day, and we never get any closer to anything except Death. Look at how you write about us, and talk about us in Parliament. Look how you are always right and we are always wrong. Who can look at all that, Sir, and say that things are as they should be?'

'Well then,' answered Mr Bounderby, looking at Mr Harthouse and then back at Stephen. 'Perhaps you'll let this gentleman know how you would like to put things right.'

'I don't know, Sir. It's not for me to say.'

Stephen looked back at Louisa for a moment, and saw her eyes move, warningly, towards the door. He put his hand on the lock, but then decided to finish what was on his mind.

'Sir, I have little education, and cannot tell the gentleman what will put things right. But I can tell him what will never do it. The strong hand will never do it. Making one side always right and the other side always wrong will never do it. Leaving a great, black world between the two sides will never do it. Treating us like numbers on a page, or machines in a factory; without loves or likes, without hearts or hopes – that, Sir, will never do it.'

'You are trouble, Blackpool!' cried Mr Bounderby, the wind now very stormy indeed. 'Always making trouble! Always complaining! Even your own Union men want nothing to do with you. I never thought I'd agree with them about anything, but they're right about you. I'll have nothing to do with you either. You can finish the piece of work you're doing, and then you can go somewhere else!'

'Sir,' said Stephen looking up at him. 'You know that if I can't get work with you, I can't get it anywhere else.'

But Mr Bounderby made it clear that he had nothing more to say to him. Louisa's eyes were now **lowered**. Stephen put on his hat, and left the house

Night was falling when Stephen closed the big black door behind him, and went down the two white steps to the street. He had walked a short way down the darkening street when he heard footsteps behind him, and turned around. To his surprise, he saw the same **cheerful** old woman he had met on his last visit to the same house. She was talking to Rachael.

'Here I am again, you see,' said the old woman, turning to Stephen. 'I read in the newspaper that Mr Bounderby was married, and I've been waiting here all day to see his wife.'

Although she seemed a simple, honest woman, there was something about her which Stephen recognized, and did not like. Still, he tried to be as kind to her as he could.

'I've seen the lady,' he told her. 'And she was young and handsome, with fine, dark, thinking eyes. She had a still way, like I've never seen before.'

'Young and handsome!' cried the old woman, **overjoyed**. 'And what a happy wife!'

'I suppose she is,' he replied, but his voice was far from **certain**.

'Suppose?' repeated the woman. 'But she must be happy! She's your employer's wife!'

'He's not my employer any more,' said Stephen. 'It's finished between him and me.'

lower to make something go down

cheerful happy

overjoyed very happy

certain sure

'Have you left his factory, Stephen?' asked Rachael quickly and anxiously. 'But where will you go?'

'I don't know tonight. But it'll be better for you when I've gone, Rachael. And don't worry, my heart's lighter now.'

She answered him with her comforting smile. The three walked on together, and went up to Stephen's room.

'I've never asked your name,' said Stephen to the woman, as they sat together with a simple supper of tea and bread.

'Mrs Pegler,' she replied cheerfully. 'I'm a **widow**. My dear husband – one of the best – died many years ago, and I'm all alone now.'

'No children, then?' he asked.

'No, not now,' she answered in a shaking voice. 'I once had a son. He did well, wonderfully well. But – I have lost him.'

Just then, the woman who owned the shop below came up the stairs, and whispered a few words into Stephen's ear.

'Bounderby!' cried Mrs Pegler, who had caught a word of what the woman had whispered. 'Hide me! Oh, hide me!' and she disappeared into a dark corner of the room.

A moment later, Louisa entered the room, followed by Tom.

'I have come to speak to you, Mr Blackpool, because of what has just happened,' she said. 'I would like to help you, if you will let me. Tell me, what will you do now?'

'Well, Madam,' he replied. 'When I've finished, I'll go and look for work somewhere else. It won't be easy, but I'll try.'

Louisa blushed, and took a ten pound note from her purse. 'This is for you, to help you on your way.'

widow a woman whose husband is dead

'I am grateful for your kindness. I'll borrow two pounds, and paying it back will be the sweetest work I've ever done, Madam.'

Until this moment, Tom had been sitting on the bed, looking bored. As he saw Louisa getting ready to leave, he jumped up. 'Wait, Loo! I want to speak to him a moment. Step out on the stairs, Blackpool. Don't bring a light!'

Stephen followed him out to the darkened stairs.

'Look here!' whispered Tom, his hot face close to Stephen's. 'I think I can do something to help you. When are you leaving Coketown?'

'In about three or four days' time,' replied Stephen.

'Three or four days,' repeated Tom, pushing his finger into the buttonhole of Stephen's coat, and turning it. 'Now, could you recognize the man who brought you the message tonight?'

Stephen said that he could.

'Well,' went on Tom, his words coming out hurriedly and anxiously. 'For the next few nights, when you leave work, just stand around outside the Bank for about an hour, will you? That man might give you a note or something. Let him see you, but don't speak to him. Do you understand?'

'Yes, Sir, I understand,' said Stephen.

With that, Tom called to his sister, and the visitors left. Stephen and Rachael took Mrs Pegler to the station, then said a last goodbye to each other at the corner of Rachael's street.

For the next three days Stephen did his lonely work at the factory, and each evening he stood for an hour or more in the darkness outside the Bank, but no one brought a note. Early on the fourth day, he packed his bags and stepped out into the quiet, sleeping streets. As the sun appeared in the **pale** sky, he climbed up into the countryside, leaving the silent factories and tall chimneys far below him. The morning was clear and bright, and the trees above his head whispered that he left behind him a true and loving heart.

pale without a lot of colour

READING CHECK

Tick (✔) the correct answers.

a Why does Slackbridge come to Coketown?

  1 ☐ Because he wants Stephen Blackpool to lose his job.

  2 ☐ Because he wants the workers there to join the Union.

  3 ☑ Because he wants to fight the workers.

b Why does Stephen tell Mr Bounderby what he thinks?

  1 ☐ Because he's very afraid of the Union.

  2 ☐ Because he doesn't like Slackbridge or agree with what he is doing.

  3 ☐ Because Louisa looks at him in a friendly way.

c Why does Mr Bounderby tell Stephen to leave his factory?

  1 ☐ Because he doesn't like what Stephen says.

  2 ☐ Because he's a member of the Union.

  3 ☐ Because the Union people don't like him.

d Why does Mrs Pegler visit Coketown again?

  1 ☐ Because she likes Mr Bounderby's wife.

  2 ☐ Because she read about Mr Bounderby's marriage in a newspaper.

  3 ☐ Because Stephen and Rachael invite her to supper.

e Why does Louisa go to visit Stephen Blackpool?

  1 ☐ Because she wants to help him.

  2 ☐ Because Tom wants to speak to him.

  3 ☐ Because she wants to give him a new job.

f What does Tom want Stephen to do?

  1 ☐ To give him some money.

  2 ☐ To take a note to Bitzer in the Bank.

  3 ☐ To wait for Bitzer outside the Bank.

WORD WORK

Find words in the bricks to complete the sentences.

a Most of the workers decide that they want to be in the _Union_ .

b Slackbridge has a _ _ _ _ _ _ voice because he speaks a lot.

c He lifts his _ _ _ _ in the air when he is angry.

d When Stephen hears Bitzer speaking to him, he _ _ _ _ _ _ _ .

e In the early morning the sky is very _ _ _ _ _ .

f Mrs Pegler's husband is dead, so she's a _ _ _ _ _ _ .

g Mrs Pegler is a very _ _ _ _ _ _ _ _ _ old lady.

h Louisa _ _ _ _ _ _ her eyes when Stephen loses his job.

i Mr Bounderby says that his workers are always _ _ _ _ _ _ _ _ _ _ _ _ _ .

j Mrs Pegler is _ _ _ _ _ _ _ _ _ _ to hear about Mr Bounderby's wife.

k Stephen is not _ _ _ _ _ _ _ _ that Louisa is a very happy wife.

Bricks: noniu, erasho, tsif, hlsebus, elpa, woiwd, rehelufc, roelws, aipnolcigmn, yovrejeod, tencira

GUESS WHAT

What happens in the next chapter? Match the people and the sentences.

Mr Harthouse **Bitzer** **Tom** **Mr Bounderby**

a .... talks to Louisa about Tom's money problems.

b .... tells Mr Harthouse that some money has gone from the Bank.

c .... gives Tom some money.

d .... usually locks the Bank at night.

e .... tells Mr Harthouse that people believe Stephen Blackpool robbed the Bank.

f .... doesn't want to talk to Louisa about the money disappearing from the Bank.

41

Chapter 7
A robbery at the Bank

Mr Bounderby had managed to buy a very grand country house with its own large grounds, about fifteen miles from the town. It had belonged to a rich man whose business had fallen on hard times, and the bank had taken the house from him. Mr Bounderby now lived among this man's fine paintings and beautiful furniture, while telling anyone who was ready to listen that he cared nothing for these grand things. He also invited the gentleman, Mr Harthouse, to his home as often as possible, although he cared nothing for people from grand families either.

Mr Harthouse himself was more than happy to be a visitor at the Bounderbys'. He had begun to think that he'd like it if the pretty but impassive face, which changed so beautifully for the sullen young brother, could change for him, too.

'Mrs Bounderby, how lucky I am to find you alone here,' he said to Louisa, finding her one afternoon among the leafy shadows of the woods near the house.

There was no luck at all about this meeting, for he knew that she was always alone at this time of day, and that this was her favourite place. She often sat there watching last year's fallen leaves, as she had watched the dying fire at her father's home.

'Your brother, my good friend Tom,' he began, sitting down beside her, and seeing her face brighten up at those words. 'I am worried about him. Tell me, do you think he gambles?'

'I think he does, Mr Harthouse,' she said, and Harthouse waited.

'I know he does,' she added after a moment.

'And does he lose?' asked Mr Harthouse.

'Yes,' she replied.

'Mrs Bounderby, I fear Tom is in trouble. Please be honest with me. Has he borrowed much money from you?'

'When I married, I found Tom had large **debts**. To pay them,

debt money that you must pay back to someone

I sold a few – a few things which weren't worth anything to me.'

She stopped for a moment, and blushed. Did Mr Harthouse know that she spoke of her husband's presents?

'Since then he has often asked me for money, and I have given him what I could. But recently he has been asking for more than a hundred pounds at a time, and I have not been able to give it to him. I have told nobody else this secret.'

'There is one thing for which I cannot forgive your brother,' said Harthouse. 'I cannot **forgive** him for the way he treats his best friend. She gives him endless love and kindness, and he pays her back with his sullen, selfish, and ungrateful ways. My dearest wish is to help him, and to change these ways.'

Tears suddenly filled Louisa's eyes, and she took Harthouse's hand in hers for a moment.

forgive (*past* **forgave**, **forgiven**) to stop being angry with someone for something bad that they did

tear water that comes from your eye when you cry

fool a stupid person

robbery taking something that is not yours

false not real

'Look, here comes your brother now,' said Mr Harthouse.

Tom was walking along, angrily hitting the trees with his stick. Harthouse put his arm around Tom, and the three of them returned to the house. Louisa went in, and Harthouse invited Tom to walk with him in the flower garden, not far from Louisa's window. Maybe she could even see them there.

'Tom, my friend, what's the matter?'

'Oh, Mr Harthouse!' cried Tom. 'You've no idea of the trouble I'm in. It's trouble my sister could get me out of, but she won't.'

'But Tom, if your sister hasn't got the money—'

'She could get it from old Bounderby. She married him to help me, so she should get it for me, shouldn't she?' said Tom miserably, pulling the heads from some flowers and biting them.

'Dear Tom, let me be your banker. How much do you need?'

'Oh, Mr Harthouse, you're a true friend!'

'You stupid **fool**!' thought Harthouse, as Tom began to cry.

'There's something you can do for me,' he said kindly. 'I'd really like you to be softer and more loving towards your sister.'

'I will, Mr Harthouse,' promised Tom gratefully.

That evening at dinner he was indeed a kinder and gentler brother to Louisa. And after that there was a smile on Louisa's face for someone else.

Very pleased that the first steps of his adventure were going so well, Mr Harthouse rode back to the Bounderbys' next evening. He was about half a mile from the house when Bounderby suddenly jumped out into the road in front of him.

'Harthouse!' he cried, his face red and shining. 'Have you heard? There was a **robbery** at the Bank last night! With a **false** key!'

'Really?' replied James Harthouse. 'How did it happen?'

Louisa then came up, with Mrs Sparsit and Bitzer. Louisa looked very white, and Harthouse gave her his arm.

'Well,' began Mr Bounderby. 'At the end of business hours yesterday, this lady (and she is a lady) Mrs Sparsit, and young Bitzer here, locked everything away as usual. In the little **safe** in young Tom's office there was just over a hundred and fifty pounds. But while the good lady and the young man slept, people broke into this safe, took the money and then left by the front door. They locked it behind them with a false key, which was picked up at midday, outside the Bank!'

'Is anybody **suspected**?' asked Mr Harthouse.

'Suspected?' repeated Bounderby. 'Somebody is indeed suspected! And that somebody is a Hand.'

'I hope,' said Harthouse lazily, 'it's not our friend Black—'

'Blackpool, Sir,' said Bounderby. 'That's the man. Oh yes! I knew he was a bad one. He was seen, night after night, outside the Bank. And then what did he do? He ran away, just like my own mother did. And he wasn't alone. There was an old woman who watched my house all day, to report what she'd seen to Blackpool. She left Coketown with him. We'll get them both in the end, don't you worry.'

That night Louisa went to her brother's room.

'My dear Tom,' she said. 'Have you anything to tell me?'

'I don't know what you mean, Loo,' he answered.

'Please, Tom, I'll be true to you. Nothing that you say will change me. Just whisper "Yes" and I'll understand you.'

She turned her ear to his lips, but he stayed silent.

'Tom,' she said. 'Have you told anyone that we went to that man's home, or that we saw those three people together?'

'No. Didn't you ask me to keep it quiet?'

'Yes, but I did not know then what was going to happen.'

'Neither did I,' said Tom, a little too quickly.

He then kissed Louisa sleepily, and wished her goodnight.

safe a box with a lock where you put important or expensive things

suspect to think that somebody has done something wrong

READING CHECK

Correct the mistakes in these sentences.

a Mr Harthouse meets Louisa one day in the drawing-room of her country house.

woods

b They talk about Tom's problems with women.

c Louisa sold some of her father's presents to pay off Tom's debts.

d Mr Harthouse gives Tom some flowers so that Louisa will think he is a kind man.

e Louisa tells Mr Harthouse about the bank robbery.

f Bounderby thinks that Bitzer took the money because he was seen outside the Bank.

g Louisa goes to Tom's office because she suspects that he knows something about the robbery.

h Tom tells Louisa everything.

WORD WORK

Use the words in the smoke to complete Louisa's diary on page 47.

false

safe

~~debts~~

forgive

fool

suspect

tears

robbery

Thursday

I'm afraid Tom has lots of **a)** ___debts___ . *He is a* **b)** _____
about money. Of course I **c)** _____ *him for that. I have always*
forgiven him for everything. But this **d)** _____ *at the bank is*
very strange. They say that a **e)** _____ *key was used to open*
the **f)** _____ *in Tom's office and take all the money out, but I*
don't believe it. I'm afraid that I **g)** _____ *Tom, but he hasn't*
said anything to me about it. Why are there **h)** _____ *in my*
eyes as I am writing this?

GUESS WHAT

What happens in the next chapter? Tick (✔) the boxes.

		Yes	No
a	Louisa leaves Mr Bounderby and goes to her father's house.	☐	☐
b	Louisa leaves Mr Bounderby and goes away with Mr Harthouse.	☐	☐
c	Sissy falls in love with Mr Harthouse.	☐	☐
d	Louisa and Mr Harthouse meet secretly.	☐	☐
e	Mrs Sparsit moves from the Bank back to Mr Bounderby's house.	☐	☐
f	Mrs Pegler meets Mr Bounderby.	☐	☐

Chapter 8
Mrs Sparsit's staircase

Mrs Sparsit, who still seemed shaken and unwell after the robbery at the Bank, was invited by Mr Bounderby to stay at his house until she felt better. The high-class lady quickly made it her business to make sure that Mr Bounderby was happy and comfortable at all times. She made his favourite warm drink at night, played his favourite card games with him, and took the greatest care of all his needs.

As soon as Mr Bounderby was out of the room, she turned to his face in the painting on the wall, and cried 'You old fool!' But to

his own face, Mrs Sparsit was endlessly caring, endlessly grateful. Mr Bounderby soon became softer than usual towards her, and harder towards his wife. With this new hardness, Louisa found herself, day by day, growing closer to James Harthouse.

One morning the news arrived that Mrs Gradgrind, never a well woman, was now very ill indeed. Louisa immediately returned to Stone Lodge, the unhappy home where hard facts had destroyed every small, bright hope in her young heart.

With a heavy sadness in her, Louisa entered the drawing room of her old home. Her mother lay there, almost hidden under her blankets. With her was Sissy, and also the youngest Gradgrind, Jane, now a girl of twelve. Louisa had treated Sissy with coldness ever since the day of her marriage proposal, and had never again softened towards her.

'How are you, Mother?' asked Louisa.

'You want to hear of me, my dear?' said a weak voice from under the blankets. 'That's something new, I'm sure, when anybody wants to hear of me.'

After a long silence, the voice spoke again. 'You've learnt a lot, Louisa, so many books, so many books. But there's something that your father has missed, or forgotten. It isn't from a book at all. But I can't remember what it is. I'll write to your father to ask him. Give me a pen, give me a pen ...'

Thinking that the pen was already in her shaking hand, Mrs Gradgrind began to write unseen words above her blankets. Then the hand stopped moving, and the light in her, which had always been so weak and pale, finally went out.

Life went on at the Bounderbys' house, and the watchful Mrs Sparsit found a new business in life. She had built, in her mind, a great **staircase**, with a deep, black **pit** of **shame** at the bottom. As Louisa became closer and closer to James Harthouse, Mrs Sparsit's birdy little eyes watched her, hour by hour, climbing down towards the pit of shame.

One cloudy September evening, when Mr Bounderby was away in London on business and Tom was in Coketown, Mrs Sparsit found that Mr Bounderby's country house was empty. Where was Louisa? Mrs Sparsit quickly made her way down to the woods, where she hid herself among the trees and listened. Through the leaves she heard low voices. Louisa's voice and his voice. He had come secretly on horseback, and tied to a tree not far away was his horse.

'My dearest love,' she heard the man's voice whisper. 'Will you not stay with me a while?'

'Not here.'

staircase a number of stairs

pit a very deep dark hole

shame the unhappy feeling when you have done something wrong or stupid

49

'Where, Louisa?'

'Not here.'

They both turned, suddenly. Was someone hiding there, among the trees? No, it was only the rain falling on leaves.

'We have so little time, Louisa. Where shall we meet?'

Mrs Sparsit could see that Harthouse's arms were around Louisa's waist now. The rain was beginning to fall harder, and she could no longer hear their words. Then Harthouse untied his horse, and rode away towards Coketown, while Louisa ran back to the house. Now here was Louisa again, hurrying out of the house, her face half-hidden. Across the garden, a mile down a stony country road, and up the wooden steps to the railway she ran, followed all the way by Mrs Sparsit.

Resting at last, Mrs Sparsit hid in the shadows by the station wall. Rain fell in large drops from her hat and down her long nose, while dirty rivers of water ran down her dress, now stained green from the wet grass. The rain beat down, and crashes of **thunder** filled the stormy sky. Then, there was a shaking of the ground, smoke, fire, a red light, a ringing bell, and Louisa stepped on to the Coketown train. Ah! The final step from the staircase, down into the black pit below!

thunder a loud noise in the sky when there is a storm

Mr Gradgrind, Member of Parliament, was home from London for the weekend. He was working in his office at Stone Lodge, listening to the deadly 'tick, tock' of the clock, and looking out of his window from time to time at the thunderstorm over the high chimneys of Coketown. The door opened, he turned round, and was astonished to see the pale face and wet clothes of his eldest daughter.

'Louisa! What is the matter?'

'Father, I want to speak to you,' she said, dropping into a chair and putting a cold hand on his arm. 'Since the day that I was born, Father, you have given me my education.'

'Yes, Louisa.'

'I wish that I had never been born! How can you give me life, but then take from me everything that makes life worth living? Everything which makes it different from death?'

She held her hands against her chest.

'The garden which should be here was never given light, never given water. Nothing could grow – no hopes, no dreams, no natural feelings. You taught me to fight against them, with your numbers, information, and facts. There is nothing in my heart, Father. Only emptiness.'

'I never knew you were unhappy, my child.'

'I have always known it. Father, do you remember our last conversation in this room?'

'I do, Louisa.'

blame to say
that someone did
something wrong

faint to fall down
suddenly because
you are weak, ill,
afraid, or horrified

'When you told me of my proposal of marriage, my mind was deadened. I hoped that by accepting this loveless marriage I could, at least, be useful to Tom. But for myself, my only comfort was to think that life soon passes, and that nothing is worth the pain and trouble of fighting.'

'Oh, my poor child,' cried the father, his head in his hands.

'I do not **blame** you, Father. That is not why I have come. I am here for another reason.'

'Tell me, my child. What can I do?'

'Father, by chance I have come to know another man, a man of the world, a man with light and easy ways. He understood me. Like me, he too cared for nothing in life. I only wondered how he cared so much for me.'

Mr Gradgrind continued to hold his daughter in his arms. He felt her body weakening, and saw a wild fire in her eyes.

'Tonight he said that he loved me, and this minute he is waiting for me. I do not know if I love him – maybe I do. I do not know if I am sorry, or if I am ashamed. All I know is that your teaching will not save me. Now, Father, you have brought me to this. Save me some other way!'

Her father held her, but she cried in a terrible voice, 'Let me go!' and she **fainted** at his feet.

The next morning Louisa woke in her old bed, in her old room at home. She was very weak, and her head was painful and heavy. Opening her eyes slowly, she saw her little sister Jane's shining, open face beside her.

'When was I brought to this room?' she asked her sister.

'Last night. Sissy brought you here,' answered little Jane. 'Louisa, Father wishes to see you. Shall I fetch him?'

'If you wish,' replied Louisa, kissing her sister. 'How bright your face is, Jane!'

'Is it? That must be because of Sissy.'

Mr Gradgrind came in, looking tired and anxious.

'My dear Louisa, my poor daughter,' he said in a shaking voice. 'Please understand, I have only meant to do right.'

'I know, Father. I have never blamed you, and never will.'

'Lately I have often been away from home, and your sister has spent much time with a person from a very different way of life,' began Mr Gradgrind quietly and uncertainly. 'Tell me, Louisa, do you think that this has done her good?'

'If my sister has been able to find a happiness inside her, then I am pleased for her. She is luckier than I am,' replied Louisa.

'My child, I feel that a change has been happening around me in this house – that what the Head could not do, perhaps the Heart has been doing silently. Could this be true?'

Louisa did not answer her father, and he left the room. She closed her eyes again. After a short while she felt there was another person by her side, and a soft hand wiped her **forehead**.

forehead the part of your face above your eyes

'Will you let me stay with you?' asked Sissy's gentle voice.

'Do you know what I am?' replied Louisa. 'I am hardened, angry, and unfair to everyone and to myself. Everything is stormy and dark to me. Do you not mind?'

'No, Louisa. I have always loved you.'

'Oh, Sissy, forgive me, have pity on me, help me! Let me rest my head on a loving heart!'

'Rest it here,' cried Sissy, taking Louisa in her arms. 'Rest it here, my dear.'

READING CHECK

1 What do they say? Complete the sentences.

1 'There's something that your father has missed, or forgotten.'

2 'I never knew you were unhappy.'

3 'You old fool!'

4 'How can you give me life, but then take from me everything that makes life worth living?'

5 'My dearest love, will you not stay with me a while?'

6 'Will you let me stay with you?'

7 'Sissy brought you here.'

a Mrs Sparsit says to Mr Bounderby's picture: 3 'You old fool!'

b ...., says Mrs Gradgrind just before she dies.

c Mr Harthouse says to Louisa: ....

d ...., says Louisa to her father.

e ...., says Mr Gradgrind to Louisa.

f ...., says little Jane Gradgrind to Louisa.

g Sissy says to Louisa when she is ill in bed: ....

2 Put these sentences in order. Number them 1–6.

a ☐ Mrs Gradgrind is ill and dies.

b 1 Mrs Sparsit is helpful at Mr Bounderby's house.

c ☐ Sissy cares for Louisa.

d ☐ Louisa goes to stay with her father.

e ☐ Louisa grows closer to James Harthouse.

f ☐ Mrs Sparsit sees Louisa and Harthouse meeting.

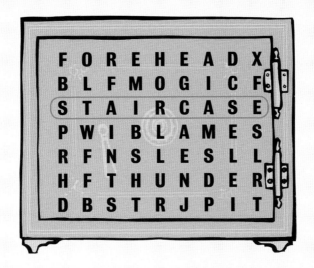

WORD WORK

1 Find words from Chapter 8 in the safe.

```
F O R E H E A D X
B L F M O G I C F
S T A I R C A S E
P W I B L A M E S
R F N S L E S L L
H F T H U N D E R
D B S T R J P I T
```

2 Complete the sentences with words from Activity 1.

a Mrs Sparsit likes to think that Louisa is walking down a ...*staircase*... with a large black .... at the bottom.

b At Stone Lodge Louisa .... and falls to the ground at her father's feet.

c It is raining and suddenly there is the noise of .... in the air.

d Sissy wipes Louisa's .... with her hand.

e Louisa doesn't .... her father for what has happened.

GUESS WHAT

What happens in the next chapter? Match the two parts of these sentences.

a Sissy visits Mr Harthouse and tells him ...

b Mr Gradgrind tells Mr Bounderby ...

c Rachael tells Mr Bounderby ...

d Mr Bounderby tells Mr Gradgrind ...

1 that she has met Tom and Louisa before.

2 that Louisa is going to stay at his house.

3 that he can keep Louisa.

4 to leave Coketown on the next train.

A night and a day passed, but still James Harthouse heard no word from Louisa. Where was she? As another night was falling and Harthouse anxiously walked up and down his hotel room, there was a knock at the door.

'Excuse me, Sir,' said a waiter's voice. 'There is a young lady here who wishes to see you.'

Harthouse threw open the door, and saw a woman who he had never met before. She was young and **plainly** dressed.

'Sir,' she began, sitting down in the chair which he offered her. 'Can I ask for your promise, as a gentleman, that you will tell no one about what I am going to say?'

'You have my promise,' he replied.

'What pretty eyes!' he thought. 'So young, but so quietly sure of herself!'

'I think you have already guessed who I have just left,' she continued in her calm, serious voice.

'The lady I have been so anxious about—'

'I left her less than an hour ago, at her father's house,' said Sissy. 'And you can be sure you'll never see her again.'

'Did the lady send you here with these hopeless words?'

'She sends no message.'

That calm, young voice, those serious eyes – for the first time in his life, James Harthouse did not know what to say.

'Can I think that there is maybe some hope that—?'

'There is no hope, Sir,' replied Sissy. 'After all the damage you have done, the only thing you can do now is to leave. You must leave tonight and never return.'

'This is **ridiculous**,' he thought, walking up and down, feeling foolish. 'But there really is no other way, no other way.'

He agreed to do as the young woman said, and she left, a smile on her calm, pretty face. An hour later James Harthouse was on

plainly simply

ridiculous very stupid

a train to London, riding through the night, feeling ridiculous, a **failure**, and very ashamed indeed.

At that same time, another train was arriving from London, carrying Mr Bounderby and Mrs Sparsit. The old lady, still wet and shaking, had hurried down to London and found her employer in his hotel. There she had exploded with news of what she had seen and **overheard**, before fainting at Bounderby's feet. Bounderby had then thrown cold water on her face and pulled her into the next Coketown train.

The pair went straight to Stone Lodge. By the time they arrived, Bounderby was redder and fatter than ever, and filled with hot air that was ready to explode at any moment, while poor Mrs Sparsit was quite hoarse and really more dead than alive.

'Now, Thomas Gradgrind,' began Bounderby in a loud voice. 'Mrs Sparsit here – a true lady, don't you forget – overheard, by accident, a conversation between your daughter and your gentleman-friend, James Harthouse. And in that conversation—'

'I know what happened,' said Mr Gradgrind quietly.

'You know?' said Bounderby, plainly astonished at the other man's calmness. 'Then perhaps you also know where your daughter is at this moment.'

failure a person who does not do well

overhear (*past* **overheard**) to hear a conversation without the people talking knowing that you are there

'I certainly do. She is here.'

'Here?' repeated Bounderby, more astonished than ever. He turned to Mrs Sparsit, who was sitting, in tears, at his feet.

'Well, good lady, what do you say to this?'

The good lady was, by this time, unable to speak, and was immediately sent off home to bed.

'Well, Thomas Gradgrind, I'm not at all pleased.'

'My dear Bounderby,' began Mr Gradgrind.

'Now excuse me, but I don't want your "dear". Josiah Bounderby of Coketown is not a "dear" man, and he's not a polite man. If you want politeness, you can get it from your gentleman-friends, but you won't get it from me!'

'Bounderby,' began Mr Gradgrind again. 'We all make mistakes. I now realize we have been wrong about Louisa.'

'What do you mean "we"?' blew Bounderby's windy voice.

'Let me say, then, I fear I have been wrong about her education.'

'I agree with you there! Education! Abandon a child in the streets, like I was abandoned. Treat him hard and beat him hard. Now, that's what I call an education.'

'Bounderby, please. I had hoped that you would help me, to try to mend what has gone wrong.'

'I don't know what you mean,' said Bounderby in a **stubborn** voice.

'I have learnt more about Louisa today than I ever learnt in her entire life. I realize that I never understood her before. And now I think it will help her if we let her stay here for a while, to get better in her own time, with Cecilia Jupe to care for her.'

Bounderby's great face turned purple with **indignation**. He stood up, his hands in his pockets, and his hair standing up on his head like a field of grass on a windy day.

'Are you trying to say there's something wrong between Loo Bounderby and myself?' shouted Bounderby. 'Well, I'll tell you, there is! Loo Bounderby (I say Loo Bounderby but I wish she'd stayed Loo Gradgrind) should be ashamed of herself. She's not good enough for Josiah Bounderby of Coketown, and that's a fact! If she doesn't come home by twelve o'clock tomorrow, I'll understand she wants to stay away. I'll send her clothes and things over here, and you can keep her!'

'Bounderby, please think about this some more—'

'When Josiah Bounderby of Coketown decides something, it is decided! And he does it at once. Good night!'

And with that, he threw on his hat **indignantly**, and left.

At five minutes past twelve the next day, Mrs Bounderby's clothes were packed and sent to Stone Lodge. Mr Bounderby then sold his country home and returned to his town house.

Now that he was living a **bachelor's** life again, Bounderby worked harder than ever at his business life, and at trying to find the people who had robbed the Bank. But as the weeks went by, there was still no news of Stephen Blackpool. The mysterious old woman who had watched his house stayed a mystery, too.

One night, on Mr Bounderby's orders, large notices were put up on walls all over Coketown. In thick black letters, they gave the name of Stephen Blackpool, wanted for the robbery of Bounderby's Bank.

stubborn not changing your mind or ideas easily

indignation a feeling of great anger

indignantly very angrily

bachelor a man who has never married

Early next morning, Stone Lodge received three visitors: Mr Bounderby, with Tom in his shadow, and Rachael.

'Mrs Bounderby,' said Bounderby coolly to Louisa. 'I know that the hour is early, but this is a very necessary visit. I have here a young woman who says that she has met you and your brother before. Young Tom here stubbornly refuses to say a word about it, so I need you to say if her story is true or not.'

Louisa told her husband that she had indeed seen Rachael before, together with Stephen Blackpool and an unknown old widow, in Stephen's room, three nights before the robbery.

'Tell us, young lady,' asked Rachael, 'why you came to Stephen's room that night.'

'I felt sorry for him, and wanted to help him,' replied Louisa.

'Oh, I thought that was true,' cried Rachael tearfully, 'but now I don't know. Maybe you had your own reasons, and didn't care about him at all. I don't know, I don't know ...'

'You should be ashamed of yourself, coming here, saying these things!' said Tom's low, angry voice, from a dark corner.

Rachael made no answer, but continued to cry.

'Come now, woman, stop this,' said Bounderby.

'Stephen's written to me, from a place where he's working under a different name, about sixty miles away,' she began.

'A different name, eh? That sounds very honest!' cried Bounderby indignantly.

'But what could the poor man do?' cried Rachael, breaking into tears again. 'With the workers against him on one side, the factory owners against him on the other. All he wants is to work in peace and do what's right!'

Rachael looked at the pity in Louisa's eyes, and went on.

'I've written to him today, telling him what people are saying here – that he's a bank robber. He'll be back to **clear his name**, in two days at the most.'

'Or earlier, if we catch him! Good day to you!' said Bounderby and then left, with Tom still in his shadow.

'Rachael,' said Sissy, who until then had been listening silently. 'In your letter, did you tell Stephen he was suspected because he was seen outside the Bank? Then he'll be ready to explain it, when he comes back.'

'I did,' replied Rachael. 'But I can't guess why he was there. His way home was the same as mine, he never had any reason to go near the Bank.'

Sissy promised to visit Rachael the next night. When Rachael had gone, Mr Gradgrind spoke for the first time.

'Louisa, my dear, do you think that it is true about this Stephen Blackpool? Did he seem an honest man to you?'

'Very honest, Father.'

'Then I ask myself: what about the real thief? Where is he? Who is he?' said Mr Gradgrind, now seeming old and tired, and putting his head in his hands.

Louisa went to her father's side, and in that moment, her eyes met Sissy's. Sissy blushed and opened her mouth to say something, but Louisa put her finger to her lips, and Sissy stayed silent.

clear his name to show that he has done nothing wrong

READING CHECK

Circle the best words to complete these sentences.

a Mr Harthouse waits in his hotel for *Mr Gradgrind / Sissy Jupe /* ~~Louisa Bounderby.~~

b Sissy comes to see Harthouse *because Louisa sent her / because Mr Gradgrind sent her / although nobody sent her.*

c She tells Harthouse that he must *leave Coketown / stop meeting Louisa / never write to Louisa.*

d Bounderby and Mrs Sparsit go to the Gradgrinds' house to speak to *Mr Gradgrind / Tom / Louisa.*

e Mr Gradgrind tells them that he thinks Louisa should *stay for a time at Stone Lodge with Sissy / never go back to Bounderby / run off to be with Mr Harthouse.*

f Mr Bounderby says that Louisa must come back to him *that evening / by twelve o'clock the next day / in a week,* or stay away forever.

g One night Bounderby puts up notices everywhere giving *Stephen Blackpool's / Mrs Pegler's / Tom Gradgrind's* name as the person wanted for the robbery at his bank.

h The next day Bounderby goes to see Louisa with Rachael to talk about *the robbery / the time that they met / Stephen Blackpool's new job.*

i At the end of the chapter, Mr Gradgrind *thinks Blackpool is the thief / thinks his son Tom is the thief / isn't sure who the thief is.*

WORD WORK

Find words in the clothes box to match the definitions on page 63.

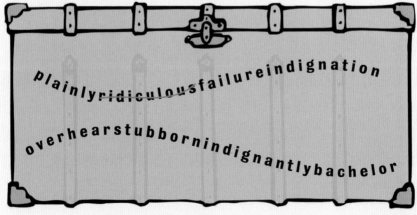

plainlyridiculousfailureindignation
overhearstubbornindignantlybachelor

a very silly, foolish .ridiculous.

b not wanting to do what other people want you to do ....

c in a shocked or angry way ....

d in a simple way ....

e a person who is not successful ....

f shock and anger ....

g to hear what someone is saying when they are speaking to somebody else ....

h a man who is not married ....

GUESS WHAT

What happens in the last chapter? Tick (✔) three boxes.

a ☐ Stephen Blackpool dies.

b ☐ Stephen Blackpool marries Rachael.

c ☐ Mr Bounderby's mother arrives.

d ☐ Mr Bounderby marries Mrs Sparsit.

e ☐ Tom goes to prison.

f ☐ Tom leaves England.

The days passed, but Stephen did not appear. Where was he? Why did he not come back? Rachael worked hard each day, and each evening she spent with Sissy, often walking in the streets to clear her aching head. One evening they noticed a large crowd of people outside Mr Bounderby's house. And to their surprise, they saw an excited Mrs Sparsit holding Mrs Pegler round the neck, pulling her up the steps to the door.

'Leave her alone, everyone!' cried Mrs Sparsit. 'She's mine!'

Rachael and Sissy were then pushed along in the crowd, through the door, and into Mr Bounderby's drawing room. Bounderby himself was there, together with Mr Gradgrind and Tom. The moment he saw Mrs Pegler his face turned all possible colours, and he exploded at Mrs Sparsit.

'What do you mean by this, Madam? Why couldn't you keep your great long nose out of my family business?'

Mrs Sparsit went white, and dropped into a chair.

'Josiah, my own boy!' cried Mrs Pegler, tearfully. 'I've kept my promise to you! I've never told anyone I was your mother.'

Mr Bounderby put his hands in his pockets, and walked up and down the room. Mr Gradgrind then turned to Mrs Pegler.

'I am surprised, Madam, that you are not ashamed to show your face here, after treating your son so badly.'

'I treated my Josiah badly? How can you say that, Sir?'

'Do you mean to say that you did not abandon him?' he asked more gently, seeing how hurt the woman looked.

'Oh no, Sir! I've always loved him dearly, and his poor father did, too. I worked hard and saved every penny to send him to school. He did well, then worked for a kind man who helped him to become the success he is today. And my dear boy never forgot his mother – he gives me more than enough money to live on.

All he asks from me is to live quietly and secretly, and tell nobody who I am. And I'm happy to do it.'

All eyes then turned to Bounderby, who spoke at last. 'I don't know why these people are here. But if they've heard enough, then perhaps they'd like to leave. And even if they haven't, perhaps they'd still like to leave. Good night.'

With that, he opened the door, and the crowd went into the street. But he knew that he looked a fool, and that soon all Coketown would learn that his entire life story was built on boastful lies.

The next day was Sunday. It was a bright, clear autumn morning, and Rachael and Sissy went up into the country, walking for several hours across quiet green hillsides.

The sun was high in the sky, when suddenly Sissy cried 'Oh, Rachael!' and picked up a hat from the grass. Inside it was the name Stephen Blackpool, written in his own hand.

'Oh, poor man!' cried Rachael, breaking into helpless tears.

They looked fearfully around, but could see nothing more. Then they stepped forward, and Rachael gave a scream which rang out across the countryside. Just in front of them, hidden by thick grass, lay the great black mouth of an abandoned **coal** pit.

'He's down there! Down there!' screamed Rachael.

They ran to fetch help. By late afternoon there was a whole village of people there. Messages were sent to Coketown, a doctor came, and also Mr Gradgrind, Louisa, and Tom. With the help of wheels and **ropes**, two workmen were lowered into the coal pit. All eyes were fastened on the black hole, as the rope slowly came up again, and a man jumped on to the grass.

'Dead or alive?' cried everyone, in one voice.

'Alive! But he's hurt very badly. Where's the doctor?'

The doctor asked him questions, and shook his head when he heard the answers. The sun was going down by now, and the red light in the evening sky lit up every anxious face.

coal it is hard and black, and burns very well; people dig coal out of a big hole called a pit

rope a very thick, strong string

tight straight

persuade to make somebody change their way of thinking

Clothes and blankets were brought to make a bed, which was fastened to the ropes, and carefully lowered back down into the pit. Night fell, and darkness covered the waiting crowd. Very slowly the wheels were turned again, and the ropes were pulled **tight**. At last the workmen appeared again, gently holding between them the poor, broken body of a man.

Whispers of pity went round the crowd, and the sound of women crying. Stephen lay with his pale, worn out face looking up at the sky. Rachael sat by him, and took his hand.

'Are you in pain, my own dear Stephen?' she asked softly.

'I have been, but it's over now. Rachael, look up there.'

Following his eyes, she saw that he was looking at a star.

'It shone on me, in my pain and trouble down below, and it made things clearer to me. I realized that it was the brother alone who did this to me, not the young lady.'

On hearing this, Mr Gradgrind moved to Stephen's side.

'Sir,' said Stephen. 'Will you clear my name?'

Mr Gradgrind asked how he could do this.

'Your son will tell you. Just ask him, Sir. I'll say no more.'

Then the workmen gently picked Stephen up, and carried him down the hillside. He smiled with happiness when he saw that they were carrying him towards the star.

'Take my hand, Rachael. We can walk together this night.'

Someone covered his face, and a long, silent line of people followed him down to his last resting place. But there was now one person missing from the crowd. Tom had disappeared.

'I sent Tom to my father's old circus,' Sissy explained to Mr Gradgrind the next morning. 'I knew where Mr Sleary always goes at this time of year. I **persuaded** him to go there, give his name, and ask Mr Sleary to hide him until I came.'

'Oh, thank you, child,' said Mr Gradgrind gratefully. 'Then there's still hope that we can get him out of the country.'

After a journey of a day and a night, Louisa and Sissy finally found the well-remembered round wooden building. Its bright flag, with the words Sleary's Circus, still flew from the top. Mr Sleary welcomed them warmly, and Sissy was overjoyed to see her old circus friends again. Then Sleary showed Louisa a hole in the wooden wall of the building, through which she could see the circus. And there, in the centre of the ring, with the painted face and ridiculous clothes of a clown, she saw her brother.

Mr Gradgrind arrived shortly after this, and made the miserable young man tell him the story of his gambling debts. He explained how he had persuaded Stephen Blackpool to wait outside the bank in order to put the blame for the robbery on him, and had then taken the money from the safe himself and left a false key in the street. Plans were made to send Tom to Liverpool. 'From there you will travel on a ship, as far away as possible, and as quickly as possible,' said Mr Gradgrind in a stern voice. The family said their goodbyes. Then, just as they were leaving, someone ran into them, and **grabbed** Tom by the **collar**. It was Bitzer, looking whiter than ever.

grab to take someone or something quickly in your hands

collar the part of your clothes that goes round your neck

'I'm sorry, but I must have Mr Tom,' he said.

'Bitzer,' said Mr Gradgrind. 'Have you no heart?'

'Indeed I do have a heart,' came his reply. 'The blood cannot travel around the body without one, Sir.'

'And can that heart not understand the feelings of others? Can it not feel pity?' asked Mr Gradgrind miserably.

'It understands facts, Sir, nothing else,' said Bitzer, Tom's collar still firmly in his fist. 'The fact is that if I take Mr Tom back to Mr Bounderby, he'll give me Mr Tom's job, and that will be good for me.'

'Bitzer, if it's only a question of **self-interest**, then maybe—'

'Mr Gradgrind, our world is built on self-interest. I learnt that when I was very young.'

To Mr Gradgrind's surprise, Mr Sleary then seemed to take Bitzer's side, and offered to drive him and Tom to the railway in his **cart**. But Sissy caught a friendly look in Sleary's eye, a look that firmly told her to stay behind with him for a moment.

self-interest
thinking about what is best for yourself rather than for other people

cart an open wooden car that horses pull

While the others went to get the cart, he told her of his plan – a dark night, a country road, a circus rider with a fast circus horse to grab Tom from the cart and take him away from Bitzer, and a clever circus dog to **bark** at Bitzer in order to frighten him and keep him in the cart until Tom had escaped.

bark (of a dog) to make a short, loud noise

Mr Gradgrind, Louisa, and Sissy spent that night awake, waiting for news. With a stern look on his face, Mr Gradgrind wrote a notice, clearing the good name of Stephen Blackpool and giving his own son's name instead as the robber of Bounderby's Bank. He planned to put that notice on every wall of Coketown.

Morning came, and Sleary brought the news that Tom was on a ship, sailing from Liverpool. Mr Gradgrind thanked Sleary with all his heart. Then Sleary took Mr Gradgrind to one side.

'Dogs are clever animals, aren't they?' he said.

Mr Gradgrind agreed that they were.

'A dog will always find you, if it wants to,' Sleary went on. 'About a year ago, an old, tired dog followed me into the ring. It stood on its two back legs, looked me in the eyes, barked, and then lay down and died. That dog was Merrylegs.'

'Sissy's father's dog!' said Mr Gradgrind.

'The very same, Sir. Well, at that moment, I knew the father was dead. I thought about writing and telling her, but then I thought: No. Why make the girl unhappy?'

'That bottle her father sent for. Sissy keeps it to this day.'

'It makes you think, doesn't it? That there is a love in this world. Not self-interest at all, but something very different.'

Sleary then called the girls to his side.

'Cecilia, my dear, kiss me and say goodbye. And you, Miss,' he said, turning to Louisa. 'It's a sweet thing for me, to see you with her, like a pair of loving sisters. Now, Sir,' he said, turning back to Mr Gradgrind, 'let us shake hands. Don't be cross with us poor travelling people. You need us. People can't work all the time, they need to be amused, too. Think the best of us, not the worst, Sir.'

READING CHECK

Are these sentences true or false? Tick (✔) the boxes.

		True	False
a	Mrs Sparsit finds Mrs Pegler and brings her to Mr Bounderby.	✔	☐
b	Mrs Pegler is Mr Bounderby's mother.	☐	☐
c	Mrs Pegler was a bad mother to Mr Bounderby.	☐	☐
d	Rachael and Sissy find Stephen Blackpool's jacket on a hillside.	☐	☐
e	They find a pit nearby and decide that Stephen has fallen down it.	☐	☐
f	People from Coketown come and get Stephen out of the pit.	☐	☐
g	Stephen dies looking at a bird in the sky.	☐	☐
h	Tom runs away to Sleary's Circus.	☐	☐
i	Tom tells Mr Bounderby all about the robbery.	☐	☐
j	Bitzer doesn't want to let Tom go because he wants his job.	☐	☐
k	Mr Sleary helps Tom escape from Bitzer.	☐	☐
l	Mr Gradgrind writes a notice saying that Bitzer robbed Bounderby's Bank.	☐	☐

WORD WORK

Use the words in the pit building to complete Mr Gradgrind's diary on page 71.

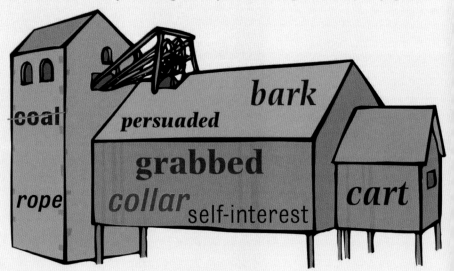

coal bark persuaded grabbed rope collar self-interest cart

Friday

They found Stephen Blackpool down a **a)** ......coal...... pit and
pulled him up with a **b)** ...., but he died soon after.
Then I went to Sleary's Circus to meet Tom. I **c)** ....
him that he had to leave the country or go to prison. Suddenly,
Bitzer arrived and he **d)** .... the **e)** .... of
Tom's coat. At last I understand that **f)** .... is the only
thing that is important to him. He left with Tom in Mr Sleary's
g) .... But when Mr Sleary's dog began to
h) ...., Bitzer was frightened and so Tom escaped.

WHAT DO YOU THINK?

1 Have you seen any films of books by Charles Dickens? What were they like?

2 Which of Charles Dickens's books would you like to read next? Why?

  a *Nicholas Nickleby* – a study of
    life at a bad school for boys.

  b *A Christmas Carol* – about
    a man who must learn that
    love and kindness are more
    important than money.

  c *Oliver Twist* – about the lives of
    poor children with no parents.

PROJECT A *A Letter from Sissy*

1 Read the letter. When did Sissy write it? Find the chapter.

Dear Father,

I miss you very badly and my life has changed so much since you went away that I still can't believe it. I don't live with Mr Sleary's circus any longer, I live with the Gradgrind family.

Do you remember Mr Gradgrind? He is the owner of the model school that you sent me to and he is a Member of Parliament. He's a very important person in Coketown. The evening that you went away I met him and his friend in the street, and they came with me to our room because they wanted to talk to you. When I found out that you weren't coming back, Mr Gradgrind made me a proposal. He said that he would give me an education and care for me but that I must never speak of my life in the circus again. I said yes, because I knew how important my education was for you.

My life here in the Gradgrind house is very strange. Mr Gradgrind is a sensible, practical man with a stern voice. He doesn't like pretty things and he doesn't think that children should have ideas. He thinks that stories and games are nonsense. He believes that we must only learn facts and more facts. I am afraid that he is disappointed in me because I am slow to learn.

I miss you very badly and hope that you will write to me soon.

With love,

Sissy

2 Match the words and phrases with the people.

Louisa

Mr Bounderby

anxious
in debt *bachelor*
full of pity
stubborn
foolish gambler
handsome **boastful**
eldest impassive
plainly-dressed
weak **proud**
extravagant
honest **simple**
selfish
gentleman
sullen

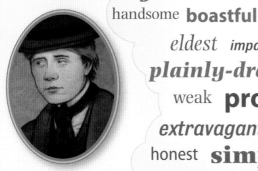

Tom

James Harthouse

Mrs Gradgrind

Rachael

3 Write another letter from Sissy to her father. Write about one or more of the people in the pictures.

PROJECTS

PROJECT B *A Writer's Life*

1 Put the life of Charles Dickens in order. Number the sentences 1–7.

Charles Dickens

a After this first success, he went on to write many successful novels. *David Copperfield* is about a poor boy who must go out to work when he is very young, and *Great Expectations* is about a boy whose parents are dead but who goes to London and becomes rich.

b Charles Dickens was born in 1812, in Portsmouth, England.

c In 1836, he began his first novel *The Pickwick Papers*, about a group of rich friends who are always in trouble. Readers loved it.

d He had a hard childhood. His father went to prison for debt when Charles was twelve, and Charles had to leave school and work in a shoe polish factory.

e He finally left school at fifteen to become a reporter writing about the English Parliament.

f He had ten children and lots of friends, but he was not very happily married. He died in 1870, aged fifty-eight.

g When his father came out of prison, Charles went back to school.

2 Use the notes to complete James Fenimore Cooper's life story on page 75.

James Fenimore Cooper

m. 1811 to Susan DeLancey. began writing aged 30

B. 1789, COOPERSTOWN (11 BROTHERS AND SISTERS!)

EDUCATION: private school in Albany Yale University (studying Latin)

d. 1851

FIRST JOB: SAILOR

books: 2nd – 'The Spy' (1821), 'The Last of the Mohicans' (1826) – one of five books about 'Hawk-eye'

74

PROJECTS

James Fenimore Cooper

James Fenimore Cooper **a)** .... Cooperstown, New York. He had eleven **b)** .... ! He **c)** .... private school in Albany and then **d)** .... at Yale University. **e)** .... leaving university, Cooper **f)** .... a sailor. He left the life of the sea in 1811 **g)** .... , Susan DeLancey, was a rich woman. Cooper looked after her lands for many years. **h)** .... at the age of thirty. His second book, *The Spy*, **i)** .... in 1821. It made Cooper famous. In 1823, he began the first **j)** .... about the wild white man 'Hawk-eye'. The most famous of these is *The Last of the Mohicans* which **k)** .... 1826. Cooper's books are great adventure stories. **l)** ....1851.

3 **Look at notes on the lives of two other writers: Alexandre Dumas (below), and Jane Austen (on page 76).**

Alexandre Dumas

began writing novels aged 37

EDUCATION: didn't get much schooling, read a lot

FIRST JOB: began writing plays in 1829

BEST KNOWN BOOKS: 'The Three Musketeers' (1844), 'The Count of Monte Cristo' (1844–5)

B. 1802, NEAR PARIS, FRANCE (HARD CHILDHOOD – FATHER DIED WHEN HE WAS 4!)

d. 1870 a poor man. spent all his money on houses & works of art, putting money into businesses that went wrong, & on his women friends

★AD's books aren't deep but they are marvellous adventures.

Jane Austen

b. 1775, Hampshire, England (happy childhood – put on plays at home in summer holidays!)

lived at home and looked after her many nieces and nephews and wrote 6 v. funny books

In JA's books the heroine always gets married in the end after many problems

EDUCATION: MOSTLY TAUGHT BY FATHER, WENT TO SCHOOL WITH OLDER SISTER CASSANDRA WHEN SHE WAS 9

*d. 1817

BEST KNOWN BOOKS: 'Sense and Sensibility' (1811), 'Pride and Prejudice' (1813), 'Mansfield Park' (1814) and 'Emma' (1816)

began writing stories aged 12 and read them to the family
had several romances as a young woman but never got married

4 **Choose a writer and write about his or her life. Use the information on pages 74, 75, and 76 to help you.**

5 **Do you agree or disagree with these sentences?**
Tick (✔) the boxes and discuss with a partner.

	Agree	Disagree
a You can understand a book better when you know about the writer's life.	☐	☐
b You don't have to know the writer to enjoy the book.	☐	☐
c Reading about the life of a writer is usually boring.	☐	☐
d I like reading about writers' lives.	☐	☐
e An interesting writer often has a boring life.	☐	☐
f Most writers want people to read their books, not to read about their lives.	☐	☐

GRAMMAR CHECK

Past Perfect: affirmative and negative

We use the Past Perfect when we are already talking about the past (using the Past Simple) and we want to talk about an action which happened earlier in the past, before the Past Simple action.

To make the Past Perfect affirmative, we use had + past participle.

The next morning someone found the key that Tom had dropped.

To make the Past Perfect negative, we use hadn't + past participle.

It was four o'clock and Mrs Gradgrind hadn't got out of bed all day.

We often use when + Past Simple in a sentence containing the Past Perfect.

Louisa had lost all hope of being happy when she married Mr Bounderby.

We often use time expressions – such as *by the time, during that time, at the time,* and *by then* – with the Past Perfect.

1 **Complete the sentences. Use the Past Perfect or Past Simple form of the verbs in brackets.**

a By the time Sissy ......arrived...... (arrive) at her father's
house, he ....had gone.... (go).

b At the time, Sissy .... (not want) to believe
that her father .... (not be) there.

c Suddenly they .... (realize) that Stephen
.... (fell) down the mine.

d When Mrs Sparsit .... (hear) everything,
she .... (run) back inside.

e I .... (be) worried about Tom because I .... (not see)
him for a long time.

f After Bitzer .... (write) his letters, he .... (speak) to
Mrs Sparsit.

g During dinner, James Harthouse .... (watch) how Tom
.... (treat) his sister.

h People .... (stop) blaming Stephen Blackpool of theft when
Mr Gradgrind .... (clear) his name.

i Mr Bounderby's mother .... (not abandon) him although that is what he
always .... (say).

GRAMMAR CHECK

Past Simple passive

We use the Past Simple passive when we are interested in an action, but not in the person who did it.

The lock was broken. The gold rings were stolen. (= *we don't know who did these actions*)

We make the Past Simple passive with was/were + past participle.

The factory was opened twenty years ago.

The workers were given very little money.

The word by can be used to introduce the person who did the action.

They were invited to the party by Mr Bounderby.

Stephen was welcomed by Rachael.

2 Complete the text. Use the Past Simple passive form of the verbs in the box.

> ask   break   ~~call~~   find   lock   give   offer   rob   see   steal

COKETOWN ENQUIRER

ROBBERY AT LOCAL BANK

On Thursday the police **a)** _were called_ to the centre of Coketown after the Bank **b)** .... The safe **c)** .... into in the early hours of the morning and an envelope with £150 in it **d)** ....

After the robbery, the front door of the Bank **e)** .... by the thief with a small key. This **f)** .... on the ground outside the Bank the next day.

Soon after the robbery, police detectives **g)** .... information about two possible suspects. The first suspect is Stephen Blackpool who **h)** .... outside the bank for some nights before the robbery. He has since disappeared. The second suspect is an old woman who watched the Bank during the day.

Immediately after the robbery, a reward of £20 **i)** .... by Mr Bounderby, the owner of the Bank, and people **j)** .... to go to the police with information.

GRAMMAR CHECK

Have/get something done

We can use have/get + noun + past participle to talk about arranging for someone to make or do something.

Have something done is more formal than get something done.

Mr Gradgrind had a school built in the town. (= He didn't build the school himself. A builder did it.)

Mrs Sparsit gets the windows cleaned by a local man. (= She doesn't do it herself. A window cleaner does it.)

We can also use have/get something done to say that something bad and/or unexpected happened to someone or something.

Stephen Blackpool had his nose broken during an argument at the factory.

The safe had some money taken from it.

3 **Complete the sentences. Use *have/get something done* and the words in brackets.**

a Mr Bounderby <u>has the bank painted</u> (have / the bank / paint) every year.

b Tom .... (get / his hair / cut) every six weeks.

c The Gradgrinds always .... (have / their lunch / cook) for them.

d Mr Harthouse .... (get / all his clothes / make) in London.

e Louisa .... (have / her photograph / take) last Tuesday.

4 **Complete the sentences. Use *have/get something done* and the words in brackets. Then look back at the book and write True or False.**

a Louisa and Harthouse (have / their conversation / overhear) by Mrs Sparsit.

<u>Louisa and Harthouse had their conversation overheard by Mrs Sparsit.</u> <u>True</u>

b Sissy (have / her bottle of Nine Oils / take) by Mr Gradgrind.

c Tom (have / his collar / grab) by Mr Bitzer at the circus.

d Mr Gradgrind (have / his house / burn down) by his son Tom.

GRAMMAR CHECK

So and neither

We can use so or neither in conversations to agree with something that someone has just said. We use so to agree with an affirmative sentence.

'I enjoy going to the circus.' 'So do I.'

We use neither to agree with a negative sentence.

'He's not interested in emotions.' 'Neither are his children.'

We use so/neither + auxiliary verb/main verb *be* + subject.

'She enjoyed meeting in secret.' 'So did he.'

'Mr Gradgrind was sad that Tom was the thief.' 'So was Louisa.'

5 **Complete the dialogues with *so* or *neither* and an auxiliary verb or the verb *be* in the correct tense.**

a **Rachel:** Stephen! I can't live like this any longer.

   Stephen: No. ..Neither can.. I. I want to marry you now.

b **Mr Gradgrind:** I think that the children need to learn facts and more facts!

   Schoolteacher: Yes, Mr Gradgrind. .... I.

c **Louisa:** I was sure that Stephen Blackpool didn't do the robbery.

   Sissy Jupe: Yes. .... I.

d **Mr Gradgrind:** Tom only thinks about himself.

   Louisa: Yes, Father. .... my husband.

e **Louisa:** We're all pleased that Father has changed.

   Mrs Gradgrind: Yes. .... I.

f **Stephen:** My mother didn't have any money at all when I was born.

   Mr Bounderby: .... my mother. She was very poor.

g **Mrs Sparsit:** I never listen to other people's conversations.

   Mr Bounderby: No. .... I. It's clearly wrong.

GRAMMAR CHECK

Too and enough/not enough

We use too + adjective to say that something is more than necessary.

These facts are too difficult!

We can add to + infinitive after the adjective to give more information about what we can or can't do as a result.

The children were too tired to learn more facts.

We use adjective + enough to say that something is as much as necessary.

The wine was plentiful enough.

We can add to + infinitive after enough to give more information about what we can or can't do as a result.

It was warm enough to meet outdoors.

We use not + adjective + enough to say that something is not as much as necessary.

She wasn't brave enough to leave him.

6 Write the sentences again. Write one new sentence with *too*, *enough*, or *not enough*.

a We can't understand the story. It's difficult.

The story _is too difficult to understand._

b Tom doesn't think of other people. He's selfish.

Tom ....

....

c Mr Bounderby can't hide his past. He isn't clever.

Mr Bounderby ....

....

d Louisa couldn't speak. She felt anxious.

Louisa ....

e Why don't you join the circus? You're strong.

You ....

f Look at the flowers in the garden. It isn't dark.

It ....

GRAMMAR CHECK

Less/the least and more/the most

We use less + adjective + than **when we compare two people or things.**

Sissy is less serious than Louisa. (= Louisa is more serious)

For Gradgrind, emotions are less important than facts. (= facts are more important)

We use the least + adjective when we compare one person or thing with more than one other person or thing.

Mr Bounderby was the least popular man in Coketown.

We use more + longer adjective + than when we compare two people or things.

Sleary was more practical than some of the other men at the circus.

Mr Gradgrind's school teaches more facts than other schools.

We use the most + longer adjective when we compare more than two people or things.

Stephen Blackpool was one of the most intelligent men at the factory.

7 **Complete the sentences with** *less* (X) **or** *more* (✓)**.**

   a Tom is ...*more foolish than*... his sister. (foolish ✓)

   b Stephen Blackpool is .... Mrs Sparsit. (cheerful X)

   c Mr Bounderby is .... Stephen Blackpool. (honest X)

   d Louisa is .... Mrs Sparsit. (anxious ✓)

   e Bitzer is .... Tom. (extravagant X)

   f Mr Gradgrind is .... Mr Harthouse. (serious ✓)

8 **Complete the sentences. Use** *the least/the most* **and the adjectives in the box.**

   > boastful   happy   healthy   mysterious   ~~ridiculous~~   self-interested

   a Bitzer is a very stupid person. He's ...*the most ridiculous*... character in the book.

   b Mrs Gradgrind is always ill. She's .... person in the Gradgrind family.

   c We don't know much about Sissy's father. He's .... man in Hard Times.

   d Rachael never smiles. She's one of .... women in Coketown.

   e Mr Bounderby tells everyone about his bank. He's .... person in the story.

   f Sissy thinks about the interests of others. She's .... character of them all.

GRAMMAR

GRAMMAR CHECK

Suffixes: -able, -ish, and -ful

We can add the suffixes -able, -ish, and -ful to a noun to make some adjectives.

We use the suffix -able to show that we can do something with someone or something.

a likeable girl (= we can like her)   *a noticeable change (= we can notice it)*

We use the suffix -ish to say that someone or something is like a noun. We can also use -ish to say that someone or something is a little bit like something, but not very much like it.

a babyish picture (= like a baby)   *a tallish boy (= a little, but not very, tall)*

We use the suffix -ful to say that someone or something has or gives something, or the feeling of something.

a tearful girl (= a girl with tears in her eyes)

a peaceful day (= a day that gives a feeling of peace)

9 **Complete the words with -*able*, -*ish*, or -*ful*.**

  a At that moment, life didn't seem very hope*ful* to Stephen Blackpool.

  b Mr Bounderby was now a very success............ banker.

  c Louisa had a very enjoy............ time talking to Mr Harthouse.

  d Mr Gradgrind didn't want the students to play child............ games at his school.

0 **Add -*able*, -*ish*, or -*ful* to the words in the box. Then complete the sentences.**

> drink   pain   thought   ~~understand~~   warm   young

  a When Louisa left Mr Bounderby some people thought that it was understandable .

  b Here – have some of this water from the river. It's ....

  c Is that bread too hot to eat? No, it isn't. It's only ....

  d When Stephen fell down the mine, it was very .... for him.

  e How old is Mr Harthouse? I'm not sure, but he looks .... to me.

  f Mr Bounderby wasn't a very .... man. He said everything that came into his head.

DOMINOES Your Choice

Read *Dominoes* for pleasure, or to develop language skills. It's your choice.

Each *Dominoes* reader includes:
- a good story to enjoy
- integrated activities to develop reading skills and increase vocabulary
- task-based projects – perfect for CEFR portfolios
- contextualized grammar activities.

Each *Dominoes* pack contains a reader and an excitingly dramatized audio recording of the story.

If you liked this *Domino*, read these:

The Secret Agent

Joseph Conrad

Adolf Verloc is a double agent, working for both the British police and a foreign country. He pretends to live a normal life with his wife, Winnie, and has a shop in London, which, at night, becomes a meeting place for anarchists. One day Verloc is told to plant a bomb – but the plan goes terribly wrong …

Does Verloc really love Winnie, or is she just part of his cover? Can Winnie ever forgive him? Who is Verloc really working for?

The Faithful Ghost and Other Tall Tales

Selected by Bill Bowler

A 'Tall Tale' is a story that's hard to believe, and the five tall tales in this book all tell of ghosts. Some have dark secrets buried in the past, others bring messages for the living. Some are laughable, some are sad, and some are just evil.

Sometimes there's a logical explanation for the strangest happenings, but often things cannot be explained by logic alone. Either way, you're sure to find some frightening reading between the covers of this book.

	CEFR	Cambridge Exams	IELTS	TOEFL iBT	TOEIC
Level 3	B1	PET	4.0	57-86	550
Level 2	A2–B1	KET-PET	3.0-4.0	–	390
Level 1	A1–A2	YLE Flyers/KET	3.0	–	225
Starter & Quick Starter	A1	YLE Movers	1.0–2.0	–	–

You can find details and a full list of books and teachers' resources on our website:
www.oup.com/elt/gradedreaders